A Very
Touchy
Subject

A Very Touchy Subject

〰〰〰〰〰〰〰〰〰〰〰〰

Todd Strasser

DELACORTE PRESS / NEW YORK

Published by
Delacorte Press
1 Dag Hammarskjold Plaza
New York, N.Y. 10017

MANUFACTURED IN THE UNITED STATES OF AMERICA

FIRST PRINTING

Library of Congress Cataloging in Publication Data
Strasser, Todd.
      A very touchy subject.
      Summary: The summer before Scott's senior year, when
his libido is especially high, he befriends
his neighbor—a troubled girl of questionable repute—and
surprisingly develops a new slant on life.
      I. Title.
PZ7.S899Ve   1985   [Fic]
ISBN 0-385-29378-X
Library of Congress Catalog Card Number: 84-16963

To Richie and Linda, and the twins

A Very Touchy Subject

WARNING

A lot of this book is about a very touchy subject—sex. Get it? Touchy? Oh, well. I just want to say that if all you're looking for are graphic scenes of people undressing, and a lot of dirty words, you might as well stop reading now. Because you're not going to find any. I mean it. I didn't write this book so that you could sit around with your friends and giggle at the good parts. I wrote it because I and a lot of the guys I know have something in common when it comes to sex. And that is that it's been making us crazy for years.

In case you're wondering why I decided to write a book, all I can tell you is that I'm seventeen years old and for the last three years I've probably spent an average of 47% of each day thinking about sex. Maybe if there'd been someone I could have talked to about it, I wouldn't have written a book. But there wasn't. If you're a guy and you talk to other guys about sex, they either don't know the answers or they just BS you to death. And forget about parents and teachers. This may make a lot of adults mad, but frankly I think you'd have to be an absolute nerd to sit down and discuss the intimate aspects of your life with your biology teacher or someone. I mean, a guy's got to have some self-respect. I'm serious about that.

—Scott Tauscher

CHAPTER 1

Every morning around eight my mother makes breakfast for herself, my father, and my sister, Kerry. Sometimes I eat too, if I can drag myself out of bed. It's the summer now and I really don't have to get up that early because my job at the Soundview Club doesn't begin until two in the afternoon. But a couple of mornings each week I get up early to cut lawns around the neighborhood. Other days I sleep late. Especially if my girlfriend, Alix, has kept me up the night before.

Lately, though, nothing in the world could make me miss breakfast. To understand why, first I better explain that we live in what is probably your typical suburban split-level house on a quarter-acre plot in your typical respectable middle-class Westchester neighborhood. Which means that the houses around here are close enough together so that if your neighbor lets out a loud belch, you'd probably hear it.

The other thing you have to understand is that from our kitchen we have an excellent view of Mrs. Finkel's ranch house next door. More precisely, from my seat at our kitchen table I have a direct view of Paula Finkel's bedroom.

Anyway, every morning at around 8:05 for the last week or so, I have dragged myself out of bed and down to the kitchen table. But while my parents and sister eat their eggs and toast and generally act oblivious of the world, I sit and stare across the yard at Paula Finkel's bedroom window.

What I see is utterly, mind-bogglingly bizarre. Because just about every morning at 8:15 a guy crawls out of Paula Finkel's bedroom window. That's right, he crawls *out* of the window. And lowers himself to the ground. And dusts his hands off. And lights a cigarette. And takes a leisurely stroll across our backyard, cuts through the bushes, and disappears.

One other thing: Paula Finkel is fifteen years old.

I hope you can understand how weird this is. I mean, I'm no cretin. I know some fifteen-year-old girls have sex. Some even have sex at thirteen or fourteen. And something like one out of seven gets pregnant too. But those girls aren't usually your next door neighbor.

Anyway, you might think that someone else at the kitchen table would notice that I seem to gag on my waffles each morning when this guy shinnies out of Paula's window. But forget it. You could probably drive an eighteen-wheeler right through the living room at breakfasttime and no one in my family would even blink.

So I've made a decision. This morning I'm going to alert them just as soon as Romeo next door starts his escape routine. It should be a kick to see how they react. But it's still a little early yet. So in the meantime let me introduce you to this cast of characters with whom I live.

CHAPTER 2

Sitting on my right is my mother, Mrs. Activity, spreading orange marmalade on a freshly baked croissant. Mrs. Activity is your typical tall, trim suburban matron in a white tennis dress. Three days a week she teaches kids to play tennis—a sport she takes very seriously. She also organizes clinics, runs round robins, and calls lines at tournaments. Next time you're watching tennis on TV and you see some multimillionaire tennis pro screaming obscenities at a tall lady with short black hair, think of my mother.

Sitting on my left in the tight-fitting brown polyester suit is my father, Mr. Workaholic, the man who makes it all possible. As usual he is wolfing down his eggs and coffee and will have indigestion in half an hour.

Mr. Workaholic is overweight, underexercised, and a fairly good candidate for cardiac arrest. This worries my mother and the rest of our family too. We would like to see him do something besides eat and work, but as sales manager for the U.S. Matrimonial Charm Company he has this strange compulsion to be the first to arrive at work and the last to leave. In case you're wondering, matrimonial charms are those little plastic brides and grooms who spend their finest hours standing on the tops of wedding cakes.

The next member of our family is my sister, Kerry, sitting on my father's left and across from me, doing a great squirrel imitation as she nibbles at a piece of bacon. This morning Kerry is wearing a white tennis shirt and blue shorts, and her brown hair is pulled into pigtails. She is fourteen (one year younger than Paula Finkel) but at five foot six and 125 pounds, it's hard to think of her as a "little" sister.

Kerry is the star of our family. My mother is convinced she is going to be the next great teenaged tennis millionaire just as soon as she works the kinks out of her backhand and gets a press agent.

(I know you're probably wondering what happened to Romeo and his escape routine. From the kitchen clock I can see that he should be appearing in a minute or two. That leaves just enough time to tell you about the last member of the family, the guy chewing on a piece of toast and wearing a yellow Jack Daniel's T-shirt and white carpenter pants with grass stains on the knees —me.)

What can I tell you about myself? You know that I'm seventeen. I have dark wavy hair and I'm about six feet tall with what you'd call a trim build. Not muscular, but not thin either. I'm reasonably decent-looking, and the thing that everyone says they notice first about me are my eyebrows. My whole family is big in the eyebrow department. They're thick and they're long and, well, they're noticeable. For as long as I can remember, girls have told me they liked my eyebrows.

Personality-wise, I'm Mr. Nice Guy. My friend Albert (you'll meet him later) says I'm a wussy because I never have strong opinions about anything and I try too hard to make people like me. It's true. I'm the kind of person who always tries to say something nice about someone. I guess I'm that way because I'm not a star like my sister; I'm more of a sweat hog like my father. I work hard and I like an occasional beer. A real all-American guy. And 47% sex fiend too.

CHAPTER 3

Okay, folks, the moment has arrived. From my seat at our kitchen table I see a pair of hands grab on to the sill of Paula Finkel's bedroom window. As usual, the rest of my family is too busy eating to notice.

"Uh-hum," I clear my throat. "Check out what's happening next door."

Kerry looks up from her toast, squints, then grabs the ends of her pigtails and cries, "There's someone climbing out of the Finkels' house!"

We all crane our necks to watch as Romeo, wearing a black T-shirt and grimy jeans, pulls himself through the window and lowers himself to a bare patch of ground between two evergreen bushes. He's got slick black hair, and tattoos on his arms, and he must be at least eighteen or nineteen. He dusts his hands off, sticks a cigarette between his lips, lights it, and strolls toward our backyard.

Back in our kitchen my father is rising from his seat, his napkin falling off his lap to the floor. I know what he's thinking. This is a respectable neighborhood, not some low-life slum. We mustn't allow greaseball punks to plunder and pillage here.

My mother is also rising. "Wait, honey!"

Does she hope to stop him before he engages in hand-to-hand

combat with Romeo in the backyard? Forget it. This is no job for a middle-aged matrimonial charm salesman. This is a job for the police! He grabs the wall phone.

I wave at him. "Wait a minute, Dad."

He pauses, his finger in middial. "What, Scott?"

"That guy's been doing that every morning for the last week and a half," I tell him.

"He has?" My father looks confused.

My mother turns away from the window. "I don't understand."

I glance at Kerry. "That's Paula's window, right?"

Kerry nods.

It takes my parents a second to catch on. Then my mother says, "Oh, dear."

My father gives Kerry a concerned look. "But Paula's just a little girl. She's your age."

"She's a year older than me," Kerry says.

"What's the difference?" my father asks. "Fourteen, fifteen. She's just a child."

Kerry and my mother exchange knowing glances, and then my sister says, "Have you taken a close look at Paula lately?"

"Well, no, not really." He lets go of the phone and sits down again in front of his half-finished breakfast.

Kerry crosses her arms in front of her. "She's got a bod."

My father scowls. "A what?"

"She's developed," my mother explains.

"But still, at her age . . ." My father's words trail off in true puzzlement.

In the period of shocked meditation that follows, each member of the family tries to figure out just what this means. It's as if the whole idea of sex has suddenly leaped out of the closet and landed in the middle of our kitchen table, where it sits licking its sharp claws and daring my parents to try to remove it.

I don't know what they're thinking, but I don't think there's much doubt about why this guy crawls out of Paula's window in the morning. It's because he doesn't want anyone else in the house to know he's spending the night there. And by anyone else, I mean Mrs. Finkel, since Mr. Finkel ran off with another woman a couple of years ago. Furthermore, it doesn't exactly take a genius to figure out that whatever that guy is doing in Paula's bedroom every night, it isn't helping her with her homework.

"Do you think I should talk to Mrs. Finkel?" my mother asks, pouring herself a second cup of coffee.

"Yes, absolutely," says my father, a firm believer that parents still rule the world.

"What makes you think it's any of our business?" I ask.

My father turns to me. "Are you serious, Scott? A girl that age can't know what she's doing." Again he glances at Kerry.

"There are girls in my grade who do," Kerry tells him. "Mom knows."

My father stares at my mother, who sighs. "I wish you hadn't said that, Kerry."

"Girls in Kerry's grade?" my father asks. "Why haven't you told me?"

"Because I knew you'd react this way," my mother says regretfully.

"You're damn right I would." Now he turns to Kerry. "I suggest you start thinking about private school for next year."

"Oh, Dad!" Kerry wails.

"You'll have to send her to a nunnery," I tell him.

"Scott's right, dear," my mother says. "And you could have some faith in your daughter too."

"Well, it just seems like an unhealthy atmosphere to go to school in," my father says, backing off a little. He probably just remembered what private school costs.

"I don't think it's any different anywhere else," my mother says.

My father turns back to the cold remains of his breakfast. It's not that he and my mother have never talked to Kerry and me about sex. My father sat down and explained it all to me when I was thirteen. He even had a book with diagrams. I'm pretty sure my mother went through the same routine last year with Kerry. And every so often she fills us in with little updates, like what's new in Herpesville, and that freaky disease AIDS. It's just that the attitude about sex in our house has always been that it was something that happened in the next town over. Not in this community. Not next door. And definitely not here.

CHAPTER 4

For as long as I can remember I've had jobs. No one ever had to force me to get them. It's just been natural. The first job I ever gave myself, when I was eight, was Community Undertaker for Small Animals. I went to every house on our block and announced that if they had any dead pets or other small creatures they should call me and I would come and remove the body and give it a proper burial. The only things I would not accept were insects and slugs. Then I went home and laid out a little cemetery in my backyard and made small headstones out of clay. People actually did call with dead parakeets and hamsters and birds that had flown into windows, and I probably could have kept that job for a long time, except that my mother decided it wasn't healthy for me to handle all those dead animals. She made me stop.

Since then I've had all the usual suburban jobs: baby-sitting, gardening, snow shoveling, leaf raking. Plus, every summer since I was thirteen I've worked at the Soundview Club. This summer I actually have two jobs. I cut lawns in the mornings and work as a valet parker at the club in the afternoons and evenings. When the summer is over, I'm going to buy a decent car.

This morning I have two lawns to do. Cutting grass is a strange business. There is probably nothing weirder than America's attitude toward its lawns. The marriage can be on the rocks, the old man out of work, and the kid in jail, but the lawn must look good. God forbid you should be cursed with brown spots, crabgrass, or dandelions. You can cover up pimples with makeup, you can send a bad kid away to military school, but you can't hide the lawn. If you have a bad lawn, you're stuck with it for the whole neighborhood to see.

Take the lawn I do first this morning, the Bermans'. I'm sure the Bermans are nice people, but they're potential suicides as far as their lawn is concerned. It's not their fault that they have a lot of shade trees and that the grass won't grow well under them. It's not their fault that big ugly tree roots stick up through the grass, and that there are brown slimy spots. That's just life, right?

But every week Mrs. Berman greets me with a list of complaints. Isn't there anything I can do about the brown spots, roots, and slime? Yeah, I can spray-paint the entire front yard green. Of course I don't say this. Instead I reassure her that I'm doing the best I can and then I get to work.

I finish the Bermans' lawn by ten thirty and head over to the Finkels' next door to my own house. Mrs. Finkel couldn't care less about her lawn. She doesn't fertilize, she doesn't put down weed killer, she doesn't water. And guess what? She has one of the best lawns in the neighborhood—thick and green, no weeds, no bare spots. It just goes to show you, the lawn gods are not fair.

As I start to push the mower back and forth across Mrs. Finkel's lawn, I think back to the events at breakfast. Mrs. Finkel and Paula moved in about two years ago, after Mr. Finkel left. But I think I saw Paula's father once. At least, one day there was this big silver Cadillac in the driveway and this guy wearing a designer jogging outfit was standing next to it, talking to Paula. They talked for a while and then she started to cry and he hugged her. A few moments later he got into the car and drove away. The rumor I heard was that he divorced Mrs. Finkel and married a younger woman.

I can't say I blame him, because Mrs. Finkel is clearly outside the realm of normality. For instance, every time I see her she's wearing a nightgown and a robe and slippers. And she hardly ever leaves her house. Instead she has all the groceries and stuff delivered and spends all day inside staring at the tube with a cigarette and a highball glass nearby. She must start hitting the juice before noon, because I smell it on her breath when she pays me.

The day's heat begins to rise around me as I cut the Finkels' lawn. My T-shirt is off and I'm sweating like a pig as I push the mower back and forth. The sun feels like it's coming down through a magnifying glass, and at any other house I'd probably take a break and knock on the front door and ask for a glass of cold water or a beer. But not at the Finkels'. Sometimes when I'm working with my shirt off, Mrs. Finkel comes to the window and watches me. She gives me the creeps.

As I push the mower past a wooden gate and into the backyard, I come to the Finkels' swimming pool. Never have its chlorinated blue waters looked so cool and inviting. Never have I yearned so to launch myself into it. Perhaps I would, were it not for the presence of Paula herself, lying on a chaise on the terrace between the house and the pool. She is wearing a small red bikini. A gold chain around her neck sparkles in the sunlight and her bronzed skin glistens with baby oil. Her eyes are closed and her ears are shrouded in earphones connected to her tape player. If she is aware of this sweat hog slaving behind the mower in her backyard, she makes no sign of it.

I push the mower onward, cursing the sun and casting secret glances at Paula. It seems incredible that just a few years ago she was a skinny, whiny kid and today she is a fifteen-year-old sun goddess with a bod and a sleep-in boyfriend. How did it happen?

One more sweep along the fence in the back and I'm finished. The skin on my shoulders feels like it's been scalded. I'm so hot, and that blue water looks so good, that I can't resist killing the mower engine and walking up to the edge of the pool.

"You think I could jump in?" I shout across to Paula.

Still supine in her chaise, she opens one eye and lets the earphones slip down to her neck. "What?"

"The pool," I tell her, pointing to those enticing waters.

Paula shrugs. "Go ahead."

Off go my sneakers, and still wearing my carpenter pants, I dive headfirst into my reward. Ah, the cool water envelops me, the chlorine stings my eyes. I'm in watery heaven. I never want to come up.

However, I do run out of air. When I surface, Paula is sitting up, pulling a brush through her black hair and watching me.

"I thought you were going to go home first and get a bathing suit," she says.

I can only crack a big grin. It is true that it would have taken me only a minute or two to get a pair of trunks. "I couldn't wait," I tell her as I swim to the side of the pool.

Paula smirks and continues brushing her hair. Now that I've jumped into the pool and cooled off, I should probably get out and go home. But something is holding me back. Could it be this fifteen-year-old girl in the skimpy bikini who sleeps with older guys? Wait a minute, Scott. She has a boyfriend and you have a girlfriend. You couldn't possibly think that she and you would ever . . .

But even as I think it, Paula rolls over onto her stomach, reaches behind her back, and undoes the strap of her bikini top. I know she does it to avoid unsightly tan lines, but my mind quickly fills with unutterable thoughts. Paula and me?

Scott, I tell myself, it's time you hauled your butt out of this pool and went home.

CHAPTER 5

My heart belongs to Alix Shuman, daughter of Big Phil Shuman, the Nissan King. Phil has the Nissan, Volvo, and Mercedes dealerships in town, and not only does Alix have my heart, she also has a bright red Mercedes convertible and a sailboat.

When I arrive home to change out of my wet carpenter pants and play back the telephone machine messages, I find that Alix has called and wants to see me tonight after I finish parking cars at the club. Alix is having a tough summer. There has been an absence of sailing companions so she hasn't been able to sail her J-24 much. As a result, she's been playing some tennis, but spends most of her time lounging around the pool, adhering to a strict tan maintenance program.

In that respect she is not unlike Paula next door. But in another respect Alix is the total opposite of Paula. Alix has my heart and she has made it clear that that is the only part of me she wants. In other words, our sex life exists only in my mind. We have been going together for nearly two years and recently I've begun to direct a great deal of energy toward convincing Alix that there's nothing wrong with a little sex, or even a lot of sex. But I haven't gotten very far, either with my arguments or otherwise.

In the meantime I feel like I'm walking around with a feverish

case of sex-on-the-brain. Before, when I saw Paula Finkel lying
on that chaise in her bikini, my insides started to twist up like a
pretzel. But I couldn't help it. It was a purely biological reaction
—in scientific terms my body is being ravaged by raging sex-
starved hormones. Otherwise I think I am a perfectly normal
seventeen-year-old male (sex fiend).

After a quick shower and lunch it's time to head for the
Soundview, one of the fanciest clubs in Westchester. This is my
fifth summer there, my first working the valet parking lot. As I
said before, it's really hot today and all afternoon we parkers
have to put up with a steady influx of cars as overheated mothers
drag their wailing children to the water's edge. We dash back
and forth from the valet shack to the parking lots, our official
Soundview orange T-shirts and blue shorts drenched with sweat,
pausing only to feed quarters into the Coke machine and gulp
down sodas.

It's not until around five thirty, after the beach crowd leaves
but before the dinner and evening crowd arrives, that we have a
chance to cool off and relax. I will now introduce the Soundview
Center for the Research and Discussion of Human Sexuality and
its current active members.

The Center itself is located on a wooden bench next to the
valet shack. This is where we valet parkers spend our free moments discussing life, liberty, and the pursuit of eligible young
women. Perhaps the most vocal member in this area is Albert,
who is sitting inside the valet shack, tenderly smoothing the
wrinkles out of the damp dollar bills he has collected as tips
today. Albert is our emotional Mediterranean lover. He is thin
and wiry with black hair that he carefully parts in the middle and
feathers back on the sides. He has dark eyes and a dark complex-
ion and wears polo shirts and khaki pants when he's not parking.
The preppy *paesano*.

Reclining on the bench outside the shack is Stu, the tall,
handsome sandy-haired Scandinavian stud. His eyes are closed as
he tries to catch up on some lost Z's. Stu is actually our valet
boss, but he's only a year older than the rest of us and doesn't

take the title of boss very seriously. Unlike Albert and Gordy (who I'll tell you about next) I've never worked with Stu before. He's kind of quiet, but he seems like a pretty nice guy.

Next to Stu sits Gordy, the short, pudgy one, the only one among us with an honest-to-God five-o'clock shadow and enough reddish brown hair on his body to keep him warm in the winter. Gordy is reading what looks like a *Time* magazine but is actually a *Penthouse* with a *Time* cover pasted over it. We have a box of these magazines in the valet shack, the covers doctored so that club members will not be offended when they see us reading them. I sometimes wonder what typical club member Mrs. Doe must think when she sees us all hunched over what looks like a *Newsweek*—"My, what nice boys, keeping up with their current events." If she only knew.

At this moment I am sitting next to Gordy, peeking over his shoulder at the pages of full frontal nudity in living color. One of the girls in the magazine is wearing (I guess I should say *was* wearing) a red bikini, and it makes me think of Paula.

Suddenly Gordy slaps the magazine closed and throws it back into the valet shack. "Why am I such a masochist?" he asks, grabbing his head dramatically. "Why do I torture myself like this?"

"Like what?" Albert asks, looking out from the shack.

"Looking at these magazines," Gordy says. "These women don't exist in real life. They only exist in magazines. It's crazy. I'm driving myself insane looking at this stuff."

"What about Mrs. Miller?" Albert asks, referring to one of the club's more attractive young mothers. "You ever see her in a bikini?"

"She has nothing to do with this," Gordy says. "Mrs. Miller is a married lady. She's ten years older than me. And even if she wasn't ten years older and married, she still wouldn't have anything to do with me."

Albert rolls up his soggy bills and stuffs them into his T-shirt pocket. "Your problem is confidence, man," he says. "When you see a good-looking girl you gotta have confidence."

Gordy smirks. "Yeah, look who's talking. Mr. Playboy himself."

"I can get it anytime I want it," Albert huffs.

"Well, then you must not want it much," Gordy replies.

"Look who's talking. Mr. Virgin," Albert taunts him.

Stu stirs from his nap. He seems to catnap a lot on the job, which makes us suspect that he's up late most nights frolicking.

"O great Norse god," Gordy says. "Tell us the meaning of life, or at least how to find an attractive girl with an accommodating nature."

Stu only yawns.

Gordy puts his chin on his hands. "Oh, God, am I getting depressed," he moans. "Another summer is here. All I see are girls in bathing suits, girls in skimpy T-shirts and tight shorts. So near and yet so far." He turns and looks at me. "And you with Miss Mercedes-Benz. I'm amazed you're not totally insane by now."

"Hey," Albert says, "you making any progress with Alix?"

"It's none of your business," I tell him. "But the answer is no anyway."

Albert shakes his head. "Man, what a waste. Why don't you drop her already? She's just a tease. All she does is jerk you around on a leash."

"Aw, leave him alone," Gordy says. "She gives him enough trouble without you."

The truth is that my pals are not particularly fond of Alix, but they forget that she and I have been with each other for two years. For most of that time we really had fun—going out, going skiing or sailing, and just spending a lot of time together. Lately, all they see is that we fight a lot, but they don't understand that for a long time we shared a lot too.

"Sometimes I just feel like I would do anything," Gordy is saying. "Anything, just to know what it feels like."

"If you want it so bad, why don't you buy it?" Albert asks.

"Oh, sure, and get every venereal disease in the book," Gordy says.

"Hey, Scott," Albert says. "What about that Paula girl who lives next to you? I heard she's a mover."

Have you ever felt like someone could read your mind? When Albert says this, it really startles me. How could he know about Paula? And why ask me about her? I know it's just a coincidence, but it shakes me just the same.

"I'd leave her alone," I tell him, thinking of her weird mother and Romeo's daily escape routine. "I think she could have problems."

"Those are my kind of problems," says Albert, leering.

"You know she's fifteen years old," I tell him.

"Trouble," Gordy says.

"Yeah? When was the last time you heard of anyone getting into trouble for that?" Albert asks. "Remember when we were in junior high? That girl Stacy?"

"Her parents sent her away to parochial school," Gordy says.

"You know why?" Albert asks.

"Everyone knows why, Albert," I tell him.

"So, all I'm saying is, Why wait until your next door neighbor gets sent away too?" Albert says.

"She's already going with someone," I tell him.

"Yeah, I know," Albert says. "The guy pumps gas at the Texaco station on the Post Road. High school dropout city."

"What's she going out with that greaseball for?" Gordy asks.

"Who knows," Albert says. "Maybe she's into the macho greaser thing. Nice little girl gets her kicks on the wrong side of the tracks. All I heard is that she isn't that particular about who she's with. That makes her perfect for you, Gordy."

"God, she's probably got every venereal disease in the world," Gordy gasps.

"You've got venereal disease on the brain, Gordy," Albert says.

I'm such a hypocrite. Here I am telling Albert to lay off Paula because she's too young, and meanwhile all I can think about is watching her undo the strap of her bikini top by the pool this morning. The thing is, I really meant what I told Albert. It almost seems like there are two Scott Tauschers. There's Mr. Nice Guy who works hard at his jobs and tries to look out for his friends. And then there's Mr. Sex Fiend and his band of wild hormones. Move over, Dr. Jekyll and Mr. Hyde.

CHAPTER 6

By ten that night the club parking lot is three-quarters empty and we four valet parkers are wiped out. Not only are we beat from the heat and work, but we've all just eaten large steak and French fry dinners, supplied by one of the dining-room busboys for a small bribe. Now, with bellies full, we're lounging around like a pride of well-fed lions, gazing up at the moths fluttering around the single bare light bulb that illuminates the side of the shack.

Next to me Gordy glances toward the clubhouse. The only members still there are the leftovers from the liquid-lunch crowd who get totally obliterated every night and then pay us good money to chauffeur them home. One of the unwritten club rules is that we have to make sure that drunks make it home alive. Actually, it's another one of the fringe benefits of being a valet parker. You can almost double your daily income between ten thirty and midnight if you get a couple of good tippers. (You just have to hope they don't barf in the car.)

We're waiting for the first casualties to start staggering out of the club bar when Alix drives up in her red Mercedes convertible. Top down, of course. She's wearing a blue Shuman Nissan baseball cap to keep her streaked chestnut hair in place and she's so tan that she'd probably get arrested in South Africa.

Somehow, Albert musters enough energy to get up from the bench and open the driver's door for her.

"Park it for you, ma'am?" he asks politely, as if she were just another club member.

"Not in a million years, Albert," she answers, taking the keys out of the ignition. "I'd like to use this car again."

Alix steps out of the Benz. She's wearing a man's white shirt (probably her brother Shawn's) with the sleeves rolled up and tight jeans and sneakers, and she walks beautifully, like a prized Thoroughbred. Alix Shuman's walk is legend. Put her on a beach or in a shopping mall and people within a 100-foot radius will turn their heads when she passes. When I'm with her, I feel like a knight escorting the princess through crowds of commoners. (Okay, so I've been accused of having a rich fantasy life.)

Alix leans against the Benz with her hands in her back pockets. Behind her Albert sits down in the driver's seat and starts playing with the gear shift. The rest of us are still sprawled on the bench.

"What's wrong with you guys?" Alix asks.

"Just relaxing after dinner," I reply.

In the Benz Albert tugs at the steering wheel. *"Varrooooom, varroooommm, brummmmbumbumbum . . .* Albert Kantana, current world leader with one hundred twenty-seven Grand Prix points has an eight-second lead on Carlos Reutmann as he downshifts through the famed S-turns of LeMans with Reutmann in hot pursuit. *Varrooooom, boom, boom.* Wait a minute! There's debris on the track from an earlier accident! Kantana has to swerve to avoid it. His Mercedes Rondeau prototype fishtails at one hundred fifty-five miles per hour. . . ." Albert twists the steering wheel violently. *"Eeerrch! Boom! Voom!* Only a series of brilliant evasive maneuvers keeps the car in control, and moments later Kantana takes the checkered flag!"

Now he vaults out of the car, his arms raised in triumph. "Albert Kantana, New World Champion!"

"Psychopath," Gordy mutters.

The grin on Albert's face disappears. "I heard that, Price. You want a fat lip?"

"No, I want a fat girlfriend," Gordy answers.

"Hey, anyone up for Fingers tonight?" Alix asks. Fingers is a dance place a couple of towns away.

Nobody responds. We're too wiped out to think about dancing.

Meanwhile, Albert points toward the clubhouse. "First casualty approaching."

We all turn and see the silhouette of a heavy man staggering down the driveway.

"Kugerman," Gordy says.

"Your turn, Scott," says Stu.

The second he says that I feel Alix's eyes on me. Kugerman pays well for chauffeur duties and he isn't one of these drunks who has to spill out all his problems to you or who becomes really abusive. But Alix doesn't want me to work anymore tonight. She wants to play.

"Let Gordy have him," I say, pushing myself up.

Gordy can't believe it. "You sure, Scott? Kugerman's good for at least ten bills."

"Don't push your luck, mucus-brain," Albert tells him. "Can't you see Scott's got better things to do?"

I turn to Stu. "Think I could take off a little early?"

"Sure."

Like I said, Stu's a good guy.

It's still pretty hot out tonight, but the breeze feels good as we cruise along the Post Road. I'm still so tired I could fall asleep right here in the car, but Alix is wired. She has plenty of energy because she probably slept until noon. She keeps playing with the radio, going from station to station and song to song. No one song is good enough; no one place is good enough. Sometimes, lately, I wonder if I'm not good enough, either.

"I'm so bored!" she shouts as we pass Cook's, a fast-food place and one of our main hangouts.

Meanwhile my eyelids are starting to get really heavy.

Alix glances at me. "Come on, Scott. Think of something to do."

All I really want to do is go to sleep. But then there's 47% of me that always has something else on its mind.

"Let's drive out to the beach and make love," I suggest.

This receives no answer. I might just as well have suggested pasting wings on the Benz and flying to Japan for breakfast. Alix believes in the domino theory of sex. It's like what they used to tell us in school about smoking pot. If you smoked it, you would automatically progress to harder drugs and ultimately wind up a heroin addict. Alix believes that if she gives in once, she will automatically start to give in more and ultimately become a nymphomaniac.

But what's this? I suddenly realize that we're heading for the beach. We go to the public beach and Alix drives across the parking lot and stops the Benz with its front tires on the sand. It's a clear night and Alix tilts her seat back and looks up at the stars. We can hear the water lapping against the shore and feel this nice cool salty breeze coming in off the Sound. My brain is sparking with possibilities. Was I wrong? Has she finally changed her mind? Is this going to be it? Circuits are buzzing from my head to my toes as I feel Alix reach for my hand. I'm sure my body temperature has risen six degrees in the last two minutes.

We turn toward each other and I touch Alix's soft hair and smell the slight scent of perfume on her skin. We start kissing. It's great and beautiful and then—

"Don't, Scott."

"Why not?"

"Because I don't want to get overstimulated."

"What's wrong with getting overstimulated?"

"Scott, please."

I'll say one thing for Alix. She's consistent. But now our beautiful moment is over. We back away from each other and raise our seat backs.

"Look, there's something I don't understand," I tell her. "You asked me what I wanted to do. I said I wanted to go to the beach and make love. Why did we come to the beach if that's not what you wanted to do?"

"Can't we just hug and kiss?" Alix asks.

"Sure we can hug and kiss," I tell her, feeling all my pent-up frustrations start to rush out. "But we've been hugging and kissing for two years, and I don't know why, but it's become hard for me to *just* hug and kiss. I mean, it's biological, Alix. It's not something that's completely under my control. Can't you understand that?"

Alix reaches over and smooths some hair on my head. "I do understand, Scott. Really. And I would love to go farther with you, but I just know that once we started we'd never stop."

"So what's so bad about that?"

Alix withdraws her hand. "Scott, I know what you're going through. I really do. But I just don't want to do it now. I've told you before, I want to wait until college."

"How can you make an arbitrary decision like that?" I ask. "What does it have to do with how we feel about each other? We've been going together for two years. You know how I feel about you. You know I'm not just looking for sex."

"I want to wait until I'm older and on my own," Alix says. "I'm not ready now and I can't do it while I'm living in my parents' house. I couldn't get up the next morning and face them. I know there are girls who feel differently, Scott. But this is the way I feel. Don't I have a right to say no?"

When Alix says that I look up at the stars. We've been over her "right to say no" so many times that I feel like a Supreme Court justice.

"Of course you have the right to say no," I tell her. "But that doesn't mean that you constantly have to say it."

"I wish you'd just accept it," Alix says, crossing her arms and looking straight ahead.

I let out a big sigh. What else can I do but accept it? For two years I've believed that just being Alix Shuman's boyfriend was reward enough. And it wasn't just because she's one of the best-looking girls around or that her father takes us on trips to Vermont every winter. In two years she's never stood me up once. And I'm pretty sure she's never lied or fooled around behind my back, either. She's always been honest with me. Someone else might make up excuses about why she wouldn't have sex. She might say she had a headache or that it was her time of the month or something. But Alix has never done that. I may not agree with her, but at least she stands up for what she believes in.

Alix fires up the Benz and starts to back up. Whatever hope we had for a pleasant evening together is gone. Is it my fault? Why can't I be satisfied with hugging and kissing? Why do I have to make a big deal over something that, in the total scope of life, isn't that important?

CHAPTER 7

The next morning I get down to the breakfast table just in time to watch Romeo make his escape out Paula's window. Dad, Mom, and Kerry are already eating, but their eyes are glued to the scene. Paula could charge admission.

Like yesterday, Romeo lowers himself between the bushes, lights a cigarette, and strolls off across our backyard. He really seems to have the air of a satisfied man. I hate to admit it, but I feel jealous.

"Does he do that *every* morning?" my father asks as I hunt around the pantry for some Pop-Tarts. My mother's rule is, once she sits down to eat her own breakfast she cooks for no man.

"Almost every morning."

"It's gross," Kerry exclaims. As usual, she's dressed in her tennis clothes. This morning she's even wearing red sweatbands around her forehead and wrists.

"What kind of girl is Paula?" my father asks.

Both my mother and Kerry stare at him, not comprehending.

"I mean, what's she like in school?" he says.

"She wears a lot of makeup and tight clothes and she's always fresh to the teachers," Kerry says.

My father nods gravely, as if this somehow explains it all.

Meanwhile, my search in the pantry has proved futile. "Hey,

where are the Pop-Tarts? I'm sure there was half a box here yesterday."

"Have you read the ingredients in them?" my mother asks.

I turn to her. "Don't tell me you threw them out."

"Yes, I did, Scott."

"But they don't have any preservatives in them," I tell her.

"They're full of sugar," my mother says.

I throw my hands up. "Great, so what am I supposed to eat for breakfast?"

"You can make yourself some toast, dear."

Unbelievable, I think to myself as I open the refrigerator in search of bread. My mother has now banned Pop-Tarts from the kitchen. They join salt, red meats, fried foods, presweetened cereals, and a load of other things that are no longer acceptable. The first thing to disappear was white sugar. If you needed to sweeten something you had to use honey. It was ridiculous. Have you ever tried to put honey on cold cereal? Kerry and I started stealing little packets of sugar from restaurants and diners and putting them on our cereal when she wasn't looking. Then my father caught us and said we had to share the sugar with him because he couldn't stand putting honey in his coffee.

But that was just the beginning, and now I've lost Pop-Tarts. I shove a couple of pieces of whole-wheat bread into the toaster and wonder what is wrong with my mother. There are so many chemicals and junk in the air and water and food anyway, what difference do Pop-Tarts make?

"Can her mother really not know what's going on?" my father asks, bringing my attention back to Paula.

"Sure, if she's drunk enough," I tell him.

"How can you say that, Scott?" my mother asks.

"It's easy."

"Well, you shouldn't," she says.

"Why not?"

"Because you don't know that it's true."

My whole-wheat toast comes up slightly singed and I start to butter it. No, I don't know for a fact that it's true, but I'd be

willing to bet it is. Just like I'd bet that I'll never see Pop-Tarts
in this kitchen again.

It seems impossible, but today is even hotter than yesterday.
It's the kind of day that melts driveways and makes little bubbles
of tar come up on the street. You don't see a dog or bird or even
an insect out in the sun. Only people. At least some animals have
enough brains to stay in the shade.

By eleven thirty I've cut two lawns and the hair on the top of
my head feels like it's about to ignite. I put the mower and leaf
catcher into my van and get in the front, reminding myself that
whatever kind of car I buy next, it better have air conditioning.
Then I feel bad and pat the van's dashboard over the hole where
the radio used to be before it was stolen. This van is my baby, my
first car. Even though it's your basic hunk of junk, I love it. I feel
guilty thinking about another car. It's like cheating on your girlfriend.

Driving home in the broiling sun. This is the kind of day
you'd like to squeeze yourself into a freezer for a few hours. As I
pull into my driveway a more practical thought occurs to me.
Maybe I can jump in Paula's pool again.

There's no way I'm going up to the Finkels' front door to ask.
Not with weird Mrs. Finkel inside. Instead I go around to our
backyard and peek over the fence to see if Paula's by the pool.
There she is, lying on the same lounge, wearing the same red
bikini, listening to the same radio.

"Paula! Yo, Paula!" I have to call her a couple of times before
she hears me and drops the earphones.

"Oh, hi." She smiles a little, but I can tell she's surprised to
see me looking over the fence at her.

"Think I could jump in your pool?"

"Uh, sure."

I go back into my house and climb the steps up to my room
two at a time. A quick change into a pair of trunks, grab a towel,
and I'm heading back down again. All I can think about is that
cool shimmering water. Well, and Paula too.

There's a gate in the fence near the back of the Finkels' house and I go through it and walk around to the pool. But Paula's not on the lounge anymore.

"Over here."

I turn around and see that she's moved to a green plastic raft in the pool. Sunning her back again. This time the strap of her bikini top stays closed. Plastic rafts are not exactly known for their stability.

"I see you changed into trunks," she says.

I grin. "How's the water?"

"Nice."

Despite the heat, it's suddenly hard to throw myself in. I stand at the edge, knowing I'll feel great once I jump in, but also dreading that first shocking moment when my body goes from hot to cold. Paula watches me from the raft. To tell you the truth, I feel a little funny about jumping in with her there. It's a weird feeling, knowing that we'll be in the water together, and alone.

I dive in. An instant of cold shock and then soothing delight. I go down deep and let my body go limp, feeling the cool water over every inch of my overheated skin. As I float toward the surface, my eyes sting slightly, but otherwise I'm utterly satisfied.

My head breaks water and I gasp for air.

"I wasn't sure if you were going to come up," Paula says from the raft at the other end of the pool.

"Sometimes I don't."

"And then what happens?"

"I sort of drown."

Paula gives me a funny look. It's kind of odd, the way we've positioned ourselves in the pool. She's down at the shallow end and I'm up at the deep end holding on to the side. We're about as far apart as you could get and still be in the water. Paula watches me. Is she wondering why, after two years of being neighbors, I've suddenly asked if I could jump in her pool two days in a row? It's a good question. There've been hot summers before and the Finkels' pool has always been here, but in the past I went to the beach or to Alix's.

"You're going to be a senior?" she asks.

"Yeah. And you're gonna be a—"

"Freshman. You were gonna say sophomore, right?"

"Uh-huh."

"I skipped too much last year and they left me back. I don't care. School's stupid. I wish I could drop out."

"Then what would you do?"

"Get a job. Move out and find a place of my own."

Find a place of her own? Wait a minute, this girl is fifteen years old. No one I knew at fifteen talked about doing that. Who would do your laundry?

"I know two girls who moved out of their houses when they were sixteen," Paula says, dipping her hands in the water and paddling toward me. As she gets closer something in my brain stirs. We are in the pool together, alone. What am I doing here? Am I just enjoying a neighborly swim? Or am I fooling around behind Alix's back? In two years with Alix it has never even occurred to me to be interested in another girl. But would I be in this pool right now if I didn't know what I know about Paula?

Paula stops paddling in the middle of the deep end. We're close now. Maybe closer than we've ever been before. I look at her face. Her eyes are brown, her nose is a little bit wide and flat, and her teeth are sort of small and yellow. She's definitely more attractive from a distance.

"What do you do at night?" she asks, bobbing gently on the raft.

"Work mostly."

"When you're not working?"

"I don't know, go to a movie or hang around with my friends." I am aware that I have neglected to mention a young lady named Alix.

"Do you have a girlfriend?" Paula asks, as if she can read my mind.

"Well, sort of," I mumble.

Paula pushes a few wet strands of hair off her face and gives me a coy look. "Sort of?"

"Yeah, well . . ." (I know why I find it so difficult to answer her question. It's because somewhere in my head there's this fantasy that some morning it's going to be me climbing out of her bedroom window.

Picture it. My mother, father, and sister sitting at the kitchen table. Around 8:15 my mother glances over at the Finkels' and sees two hands appear on Paula's windowsill. Next, the top of a head begins to come into view. Hmmm, she'll think, it's the greasy pump jockey. No, wait a minute. It's not him. It's . . . it's . . . *Oh, my God! It's my son!)*

Back in the pool I am telling myself how wrong it is to even consider such a thought. Wrong, wrong, wrong. First of all, I'm supposed to be in love with someone else. Second of all, if I was interested in Paula, it would only be for sex. Third of all, she probably isn't interested in me.

Which reminds me . . . "Aren't you going with someone?"

Paula shrugs and looks away across the pool. How come she doesn't want to talk about Romeo? A second later she looks back at me with an impish smile on her face. It makes her look kind of cute. "How old were you when you got your license?"

"Seventeen. I just got it this spring."

"That's what I want more than anything," she says. "In North Carolina you can drive with a parent when you're fifteen."

"How do you know that?"

"That's where my father lives. I went down there for a week after school ended and he taught me how to drive a stick shift. His new wife has a Fiat convertible. It was great."

"What's your father do in North Carolina?" I ask.

"He works for a computer company. He and Randy bought this beautiful house. It's huge and it has a hot tub."

"Randy?"

"That's his new wife," Paula says. "I guess she's my step-mother, but she's a lot younger than him. We're sort of like sisters." Now she has this distant look on her face. Her body may be in this pool, but her thoughts are somewhere down in North Carolina.

"You like it down there?" I ask.

Paula looks back at me. "Oh, it's okay. The people are different. They talk funny. You know, with accents. But, God, I'd do anything to get out of here. I'd move in an instant."

"How come?"

Paula gestures toward the house with her head.

"Your mother?"

"The witch," she says. But a moment later she grins at me. "Hey, want to race?"

"What? You and me?" I ask, surprised by her sudden change of subjects.

"Yeah. Ten laps. But you have to give me a two-lap lead," Paula says. "Bet you can't beat me."

"Bet I can."

"Bet you an ice cream cone," she says, slipping off the raft and into the water.

"Okay."

"But you have to give me a two-lap head start. Promise?"

"Sure."

"Okay." Paula ducks her head underwater and pushes off from the pool wall. As she swims toward the other end of the pool, I still can't figure out how we went from talking about her mother to racing. Now she turns around and heads back. I better get ready.

Two . . . one . . . *glub, glub.* Here I go. I know better than to immediately try to make up the two laps Paula has on me. Instead I figure I'll just swim steadily, catching up little by little. *Glub . . . glub . . . glub. . . .*

By the fifth lap my arms and legs are starting to get tired. I'm gasping after every stroke, and I still haven't caught up to Paula. Come on, Scott, give it a little extra umph. She must be getting tired too. You're not going to let a fifteen-year-old girl beat you.

I really pour it on, but despite all my gurgling and splashing, Paula stays ahead of me for the rest of the race. By the ninth lap I'm so tired I just want to finish without drowning. I make the last turn and practically dog-paddle toward the finish. Of course, Paula is waiting for me.

"Boy, are you out of shape," she teases, then hoists herself out of the pool and sits on the edge with her feet in the water. She's not even breathing hard.

"Hey, lay off," I manage to sputter between gasps. I'm so exhausted that they'd have to lift me out of the pool with a crane.

"So I guess that'll be a vanilla cone with sprinkles," she says.

"Who said anything about sprinkles?" I ask.

Paula starts to laugh. But then she stops short and stares behind me toward the house. I turn and look too. Standing just inside the sliding glass doors is Mrs. Finkel in a blue nightgown with a cigarette smoldering in one hand. She doesn't wave or anything; she just stares at us. I know we weren't doing anything wrong, but the way she's looking at us makes me feel like we were. Weirder still is the way Paula just stares right back at her mother. I don't know what's going on between them and I'm not sure I want to find out. But I definitely get the feeling that it's time for me to get out of the pool and go.

CHAPTER 8

Most of the time when I get home at night after work, the rest of the family is asleep. I'm usually so tired that I go right to sleep too. But tonight I'm lying in bed wide awake, staring up into the dark.

A light breeze comes in the open window. I'm covered by only a sheet. My father has this quirk about air conditioning, so the only cooling mechanism in the house is an old attic fan that is just slightly less noisy than a jet engine. But we've all gotten used to sleeping through it. That's not what's keeping me awake.

It's Paula. I know I'm attracted to her because she sleeps with guys (at least with one guy). But also I know that sex alone isn't a good enough reason to be interested in someone. You should enjoy being with her, you should like and admire and respect her, you should feel some kind of emotional caring that's different from your desire to jump in bed with her.

And something else is bothering me. It isn't just what I feel about Paula. It's what I don't feel about Alix. I don't feel like I love her anymore. At least not as much as I used to. And I don't know why or what happened. I know I used to be crazy about her. I was crazy about her from the first day I saw her our freshman year. It drove me nuts because here was this beautiful girl whom I just wanted to run away somewhere with. But I could never be alone with her. I mean, no one went out on dates freshman year. A bunch of guys and girls might go over to someone's house and have a party. And maybe, if the parents weren't there, we'd play spin the bottle or some other dumb kissing game.

(Imagine this: four guys and three girls sitting in a circle on the floor around a Coke bottle. One of the girls was Alix. The other girls weren't ugly or anything, but all four guys only wanted to kiss Alix. Every time the bottle pointed anywhere near her direction, the guy who spun it jumped up and grabbed her. After half an hour of that, I didn't want to kiss Alix anymore. I just wanted to kill the other three guys.)

I waited that whole year, but it wasn't until the summer that I got my chance. I was a lunch concession busboy and the Shumans belonged to the club. Alix came almost every day for lunch. We'd talk, laugh, fool around. Then, after I got off work, we'd go for a sail in one of the club's Sunfish, or play tennis, or just mess around in the pool. We had fun.

In tenth grade we actually started dating. Mostly we'd be together at parties, but a couple of times we got our parents to drive us to a restaurant and movie. I found out that there were certain benefits to seeing Alix. Big Phil had box seats for every kind of sporting event you could imagine. We went to football, baseball, basketball, tennis. We went up to their ski chalet at Stratton and at night Big Phil would take Shawn and us out to the best restaurants around. It was nice that Alix's parents had a lot of money, but I didn't think that had anything to do with my interest in Alix.

The summer after sophomore year I bussed the club dining room and worked late. Even though Alix had nothing to do at night, she refused to go out with other guys. People began to say, "Oh, you're the one who goes with Alix Shuman." Even adults would say it. I thought I could detect a little envy in their voices.

When junior year started last fall, I think we were really in love. Kids used to make fun of us because we shared a locker and held hands in the hall and all that stuff. They used to call us "The Dynamic Duo." There were other couples around, but when they said Dynamic Duo you knew they were talking about us. I was proud of that. I was the guy Alix Shuman went with.

So what happened? To Alix and me, I mean. What happened to enjoying each other, and to respect and admiration and caring? Our fight over sex happened. Those first couple of years it was no big deal. We liked each other, we had fun, we went out, we were the Dynamic Duo. If we didn't spend a lot of time making out, there were other things we could do. But then it started to change. If we could do everything other couples did, why not sex? There was no doubt that other couples were doing it. And more than that, I wanted to do it. I needed to do it. Those hormones were starting to drive me right up the wall.

But Alix said no, and the more she resisted, the more I pushed.

"Don't you love me? If you really loved me, you would."

"If *you* really loved me, it wouldn't be important."

"I do really love you. But it's not enough."

"If you *really* loved me, it would be enough."

These days all we seem to do is argue. And even when we're not arguing, I can feel this tension between us. It ruins whatever we're doing. We go sailing and it's there. We take a swim and it's there.

"Why not?"

"Because."

"That's not a good enough reason."

"Why do I have to have a reason?"

So here I am on a hot summer night, lying awake in bed, listening to the attic fan. You probably think that this whole sex problem with Alix is my fault, that if I'd just drop it things would be okay. But I can't. It's not just the hormones, either. Alix and I are supposed to be in love. I know it's a little early to be thinking about things like marriage, but if we're really in love, doesn't that mean we want to spend the rest of our lives together? And if that's the case, why should it matter when we start fooling around?

I mean, if Alix had some kind of moral or religious objection to having sex before marriage, I could accept that. But she doesn't. She even admits that she'll probably do it before she gets married. The reason she doesn't want to do it now and with me is completely arbitrary. She's never given me a logical answer and that's what makes me so mad.

I guess what I'm trying to say is it's not just sex that I'm asking Alix for. It's also a sign. I really need to know—does she still care?

CHAPTER 9

Each member of the Center for the Research and Discussion of Human Sexuality is working for something. For me it's a better car. For Gordy it's video equipment. I'm not sure what Stu spends his money on. He drives an old brown Chrysler Cordoba and he doesn't seem real materialistic. As valet boss he gets paid better than the rest of us, but the funny thing is, he always seems to be short of money. Maybe he spends it on these dates that keep him up late every night.

As for Albert, he's been saving for years for only one thing: a boat.

More than any of us Albert is into his image. The way he looks, the way he acts, what he has—that's all part of it. He probably could have saved enough for a boat years ago, but then he wouldn't have had any money for new clothes, or tickets to The Rangers games, or expensive dates in the city.

Anyway, Albert has finally gotten his boat and this morning, before work, he's taking us all out on it for the first time. Right now Gordy and I are sitting on Albert's metal cooler in the dirt parking lot of a marina that's nothing more than a little shack that smells of fish, a dirt parking lot, and a rickety-looking wooden dock. Still, beggars can't be choosers.

We're waiting for Stu to arrive. He's not exactly a morning

person, and while Gordy and I sit on the cooler, Albert is up at the marina office trying to call him.

Next to me Gordy is looking through a dirty, stiff copy of *Cosmopolitan* that he fished out of a garbage can. He's wearing his valet shorts and T-shirt, and I swear, every time I look at him it seems like he's grown more hair somewhere on his body.

"Hey, listen to this," he says. "You use up about three hundred and fifty *million* sperms each time you ejaculate. If you did it three times in one day, that would be more than a *billion* sperms."

He looks up at the sky. "Just think, Scott. If you had a dollar for every sperm."

I nod and look up at the sky too. Only I'm not thinking about dollars and sperms. I'm thinking that it's going to be another hot, cloudless day and, like Gordy and Albert, I'm going to spend a good deal of it thinking about girls and sex. Maybe it's some kind of disease guys get. Maybe I caught it from Albert or Gordy.

Gordy reads more: "Almost every time you sleep you have an erection." He nudges me with his elbow. "Hey, no wonder I can't sleep on my stomach. Now listen to this. It says that in prison up to sixty percent of the men become homosexual to satisfy their sexual urges."

"Bull," Albert says, returning from the phone booth. He's wearing his blue and orange valet parking clothes and a white boat captain's cap.

"That's what it says." Gordy points to the magazine.

"I don't believe it," Albert says.

"But it also says that men who were heterosexual before they went to prison always turn back to heterosexual when they leave prison, even if they were homosexual in prison," Gordy reads.

"That's a crock," Albert insists.

"Did you get Stu?" I ask.

Albert nods. "Yeah, he was still asleep, but he says it will only take him a couple of minutes to get ready."

"Great," Gordy says, looking at his watch. "That means he'll be here in an hour."

"We might as well go down to the boat," Albert says, picking up his red marine gas tank.

Gordy and I each grab one end of the cooler and follow Albert down onto the wooden docks. There are some nice-looking boats in here. A couple of long white sailboats with tall silver masts and bright blue sail covers. Some sleek speedboats and one enormous motor yacht that is so big it carries an extra boat on it.

"Which one's yours?" Gordy asks Albert eagerly.

"We're getting there, we're getting there," Albert says as he lugs the gas tank. He turns onto another, thinner wood dock. Gordy and I follow, trying to picture what Albert's boat will look like. Finally, about halfway down this dock, Albert stops next to a long black racy-looking speedboat called *The Eliminator*.

"Oh, wow," Gordy gushes. "This is beautiful!"

Albert looks down at *The Eliminator*. "Yeah, it's nice."

I can't believe it. "Albert, how could you afford this thing?"

"This?" Albert says. "I couldn't."

"You couldn't?" Gordy echoes.

"This isn't my boat," Albert says. Then he turns to the other side of the dock and points to a small blue boat with a small green outboard motor. Both the boat and the motor look ancient.

"This is my boat," Albert says proudly.

"This?" Gordy asks incredulously. "You've been saving three years for this?"

"Hey, boats aren't cheap," Albert says.

"Yeah, but this thing is the size of my bathtub."

"Well, it's not just the boat you pay for. You gotta pay for dock space and gas and insurance. It starts to add up."

"But what could this add up to?" Gordy asks.

"Aw, go to hell, Gordy," Albert yells as he climbs down into the little boat. "If you don't like it, you don't have to come." He lifts the red gas can off the dock and into the back of the boat.

"Hey, seriously, Albert," I say, "you sure we can all fit?"

"Of course," Albert says, reaching up for the cooler. "You just can't move around too much, that's all."

Slowly and carefully we put the cooler and ourselves into the

boat. By the time Albert has the gas tank hooked up and everything stowed away, we spot Stu wandering around the dock.

"Yo, Stu!" Albert shouts.

He walks over and gazes down at us, looking sleepy, his blond
hair messed up as if he didn't bother to comb it this morning.

"So this is the *Titanic*," he says, grinning and yawning.

"Just get in," Albert says impatiently.

"Where?"

"There's plenty of room in front," Albert says, clearly annoyed
with our disrespectful attitude toward his boat. The space he's
referring to in the front of the boat is a tiny seat about the size of
a loose-leaf notebook. Stu gives Albert a questioning look. "Just
get in slowly," Albert says.

While the rest of us hold the boat steady against the dock, Stu
carefully lowers himself into the front. Somehow he manages to
sit down without tipping us over, but he has to squat with his
legs around the cooler. In the back Gordy and I huddle between
the driver's seat and the motor. There is so little room that no
matter how we squirm and adjust ourselves our knees keep bang-
ing into each other. I look over the side of the boat and see that
there is only about four inches between the water and the gun-
wales.

"Are you sure this is safe?" I ask.

"Yeah, it's safe," Albert says. "You all know how to swim,
right?"

"Very funny," Gordy says.

"Don't you have any life preservers?" Stu asks.

"You know how much life preservers cost?" Albert asks.
"Look, nothing's gonna happen, but if anything does, don't
worry. The guy who sold me this boat said it's got special air
pockets so it won't sink."

"Great," Gordy says. "The boat will float and we'll sink."

"Just shut up, okay?" Albert snaps. He starts the outboard
motor and the little boat slowly pulls away from the dock. It goes
a few feet and then stops. Albert gives it a little more gas, but we
still don't go anywhere. Albert gives it more gas. The little outboard sputters and whines, but we make no progress.

"Jeez," Albert says. "Maybe we are too heavy."

"Naw," Gordy says, looking behind us. "I think the problem is we're still tied to the dock."

We all turn around and see that a rope is stretched tightly from a cleat on the back of Albert's boat to a bigger cleat on the dock. Albert throws the boat into reverse and we lurch backward and crash into the dock. Now he's really mad. He unties the rope, throws the boat into forward, and we sail away.

"Don't you have to have some kind of license before you can drive a boat?" Gordy asks as we head out toward the harbor.

Albert shakes his head.

"You don't have to pass a test or anything?"

"No, you just have to know about right of way and stuff like that," says Albert.

"What's right of way?" Gordy asks.

"It means if two boats are on a collision course, the boat on the right turns away."

"No, it doesn't," Stu says. "It means the boat on the right has the right of way. The boat on the left turns away."

Albert frowns. "You sure about that, Stu?"

Stu nods. Meanwhile, Gordy and I look at each other.

"I think," Gordy says, opening the cooler, "that it's time for a beer."

CHAPTER 10

For a while we just ride along in the harbor. Bigger, faster boats pass us and I get the feeling that some of the people on board are pointing and laughing at us four guys squeezed into Albert's tiny boat. But Albert doesn't seem to care. He keeps telling us how much faster his boat is when there is only one person in it. He even tells us we can take it out any time we like so we can see for ourselves.

The harbor is pretty big, but the waves aren't terribly rough because it opens into the Sound, which is protected from the ocean by Long Island. Albert says he could never take his boat out on the ocean, but as long as we stay in the Sound, we're safe. After a while we get out of the harbor and he cuts the engine and lets the boat drift.

"What do we do now?" Gordy asks.

"I haven't had breakfast yet," Albert says, reaching into the cooler. "Let's just hang out for a while and save some gas. Besides, we'll probably meet a boatful of girls pretty soon and tie up to them."

"What?" Gordy asks.

"That's what you do," Albert explains. "You meet another boat and tie up next to them and socialize. You see there?" He points several hundred yards across the water to three cabin cruisers floating side by side.

"Sometimes even five or six boats will tie up together," Albert says.

"Or, in our case, five or six bathtubs," Gordy says.

"Shut up, Gordy," Albert says, pulling a sandwich and beer out of the cooler. "Anyone want a brew?"

It seems kind of early to start drinking, but out here on the water there's not much else to do. Besides, we have no protection from the sun and hardly any cooling breeze. The water is almost flat, like a mirror reflecting the sun's rays up into our faces. At least a beer will cool me off.

So here we are, four guys floating around the harbor in a boat not much bigger than a bathtub, drinking beers at 10 A.M. and waiting for a mythical yacht full of beautiful women to come alongside and invite us over. Next to me Gordy shakes his head.

"This is dumb," he says.

"No, it isn't," Albert replies.

"Yes, it is," Gordy says. "This is almost as dumb as that time you made us go to that grungy bar in the city at two o'clock in the morning because someone told you that was where the nymphomaniacs went."

"It was where they went," Albert insists.

"Maybe," Gordy says. "But all I saw was two hundred other guys who thought the same thing. I swear, if a girl had walked into that place, she would have been torn limb from limb in a second."

Up in front of the boat Stu yawns and stretches one leg over the side until his foot dips into the water.

"Wouldn't mind taking a swim," he mumbles.

"You can't," Albert tells him. "You'd tip us over. And you'd never be able to get back in."

Stu shrugs.

Time for another can of beer. It seems like the only thing we can do in this boat is sit and drink. The problem is, this beer is going straight to my head. I'm not exactly a big drinker anyway, and here in the heat and sun, with the boat gently rocking us like we're in a big cradle, I'm getting real foggy in the brain. Gordy looks pretty out of it too. Stu's half asleep.

"My mother's got a boyfriend," Gordy says. "This is the first real boyfriend she's had since she and my dad separated. I'm really trying to like this guy. I mean, he doesn't seem like a jerk or anything, and I realize my old lady and my old man aren't gonna get back together. But you know what?"

"You hate his guts," Stu says, his eyes half closed.

Gordy nods. "Yeah. How'd you know?"

"I hated my stepfather too," Stu says.

Gordy finishes one can of beer and pops the top off another. "I mean, I really want to like the guy and I can tell he wants to be friendly. But I just wish he'd disappear."

The rest of us nod. Sometimes Gordy can't stop talking about his problems. Especially when he's had a couple of beers. I know we've all got problems, but I think Gordy has a harder time dealing with them than the rest of us do.

"You know what bugs me the most?" he says.

"You can hear them do it at night?" Albert asks.

"No," Gordy says. "I guess they do it, because he's been staying over a couple of times a week. But what I really hate is that she gets all the food he likes instead of what I like."

"What?" Albert scowls.

"I like chunky peanut butter," Gordy explains. "But this guy likes it smooth. So now all she gets is smooth peanut butter. And I hate skim milk, you know? But now that's the only milk she gets. Cause *he* likes it. And he likes butter pecan ice cream, right? So that's all she gets."

"You gotta be kidding me," Albert says. "If that's what bothers you, just go out and get that stuff yourself."

"I think you're missing the point," Stu tells him.

Albert frowns. "Oh, yeah? Then what's the point?"

"The point is, it would be nice if Gordy's mother still remembered him enough to get it for him."

"Yeah," Gordy says. "I mean, I know she has a right to see

this guy. It would just be nice if she didn't completely forget about me and what I like to eat."

"You know what I really hated?" Stu says. "Finding some guy's razor and junk in the medicine cabinet. I'll never forget it. I was twelve years old and I went berserk."

The rest of us nod. None of us knows Stu very well and he doesn't talk much about himself. It's sort of amazing when he reveals a little of his private life.

"Was that the guy who became your stepfather?" Albert asks.

Stu shakes his head. "It was someone else."

The boat dips and rocks gently in the water and I try to eat one of Albert's peanut butter and jelly sandwiches so that the beer in my stomach has some company. Stepfathers. Mothers with boyfriends. Weird stuff. I don't know how I'd feel if my parents ever split up. I guess I'd be pretty angry at them. Gordy doesn't seem angry, just bewildered. Stu hated his stepfather. Paula seems really angry.

A deep, throaty grumbling sound snaps me out of my thoughts. A sleek white bullet-shaped speedboat is gliding slowly toward us, and in the cockpit are three girls. One of them is wearing a black bikini. The other two are wearing one-piece suits.

"See? What'd I tell ya?" Albert whispers.

The speedboat is skippered by the girl in the bikini. She's darkly tanned with lots of wavy brown hair. She steers her boat around until she's parallel with us and fifteen feet away.

"Hey, that's some boat you've got," Albert says.

The girl in the black bikini smiles. "You like it?"

"A lot," Albert says.

The two other girls in the boat giggle. Albert stands up carefully in our little boat. He's got this big grin on his face.

"You girls want to tie up with us for a while?" he asks.

The girls look at each other and giggle again. Gordy, Stu, and I look at each other in amazement. Can this really be happening?

Now the girl in the black bikini says, "Got any smoke?"

All of us have smoked grass at one time or another, but we're not what you'd call pipe-carrying druggies.

"We got some beer," Albert offers. Then he pulls up his T-shirt. "And I can show you my appendectomy scar."

The girl in the bikini looks at him like he's crazy. Then, without warning, she throws the speedboat's throttle forward and spins the wheel. There is a sudden loud roar as the rear end of the boat digs down into the water and the front end tips up. Before we can brace ourselves, the wake hits us broadside, tipping our boat sharply. Albert gets knocked down and hits the steering wheel with a thud. Beer cans and sandwiches go flying everywhere and we all smash our knees and elbows trying to hang on as the little boat sways violently.

It's a miracle that we don't tip over. Finally the boat becomes steady again. In the water around us beer cans and sandwiches in plastic bags bob like debris after a crash. There's about four inches of water in the bottom of the boat, and every time someone moves, a little more sloshes over the side.

Albert is cradling his right arm. "Christ, I think I broke my elbow," he groans. He pulls out half of a plastic gallon milk container and tosses it to me. "Bail, man."

I start scooping water out of the bottom of the boat. Next to me, Gordy looks pale. Even Stu looks a little shaken. Albert is nursing his arm and gazing out in the distance where the white speedboat is now just a speck roaring across the harbor. "Boy, if I ever see her again . . ." he mutters.

"Right now I'd just like to see land again," Gordy moans.

Albert doesn't answer. He just starts up the engine and steers back to the marina one-handed.

CHAPTER 11

You know what kills me? Doing someone a favor and being treated like dirt for it. It's Sunday, my day off, right? So what am I doing? Am I at the beach soaking in the rays? Am I out having fun? No, I'm at the Shumans' helping Big Phil grill hot dogs for the loyal employees of Shuman Nissan/Volvo/Mercedes.

But it's okay. I don't mind giving up my day off to sweat over a broiling grill. I don't even mind playing substitute son while Alix is off racing her sailboat and no one knows where her brother Shawn is.

But I'll tell you what I do mind. I mind volunteering my free afternoon and then being treated like I'm an illegal alien or something.

Just listen to this. About three hours ago I drove in the Shumans' driveway and around to the carport. As I pulled up, the door from the house opened and The Cold One stuck her frosted blond head out. The Cold One is Alix's mother and the best word to describe her is ice.

"Scott," she said, "please park that thing out on the street."

She was talking about my van, which she didn't want parked in her carport. What did she think? That the other cars would catch some disease from it? Autorot? Clunkeritis? Heapophilia?

Jerk that I am, I did it. I'm really beginning to think that

Albert is right when he says I'm a wussy. I mean, here I am
doing her husband a favor and this is the way I'm treated.

Wussy!

Aw, hell. So what? To tell you the truth, it doesn't surprise
me. Ever since Alix and I got serious, The Cold One has made it
clear that the only reason she tolerates me is because she knows I
am not going to rape, expose to drugs, or mutilate her daughter.
She really believes that I am just a passing phase in Alix's life.
The idea of her daughter and me in a future marriage is just not
in the stars because our signs clash. Not astrological signs, dollar
signs. Alix's eventual husband may turn out to be the world's
biggest lamebrain, but if The Cold One has her way (and she
always does), the guy's middle name is going to be Bucks.

So here I am (middle name, Andrew) wearing a plastic apron,
flipping hamburgers, and doing the old substitute-son act. Sometimes I wonder why I try to be the son every father wishes he
had. I work hard, I'm always on time, I don't wise off (too
much). But if they're going to treat me like a bum anyway,
what's the point?

Everything goes smoothly and by the early evening the party
is pretty much over. The backyard looks trampled, and white
paper cups and plates are scattered around the lawn. There are
just a few Shuman Nissan employees left now, and they're standing down by the swimming pool, admiring the view of the harbor. (Alix's house is a big white Colonial up on a hill overlooking
the harbor and Sound. People call it the White House.)

Next to me Big Phil finishes taking the last of the burgers off
the Webber kettles and wipes his hands on his greasy red Shuman Nissan T-shirt. Phil is sort of fat and today he looks like a
slob in his shorts and T-shirt. But looks deceive. He's got arms
like an Olympic weightlifter, he's smart, and he works his butt
off six days a week running his dealership.

As we put the covers on the kettles, he wipes his sweaty brow
with his forearm and looks over at me. "Scott, go get us a couple
of beers." Giving orders is second nature to the Shumans.

I go over to a couple of gray plastic garbage pails that a few hours ago were filled with ice and beer. Now I reach down into the cold dirty water, pull out two cans, and bring them back to Big Phil. We sit down in lawn chairs.

"Good work, Scott," Phil says, knocking back his brew. I catch him giving me a funny look, but he quickly looks away. Bet I know what he was thinking. He really wishes it was Shawn sitting next to him. But Alix's brother would never stand around grilling burgers for his father's employees. Shawn is the original golden boy with a Porsche. He's a junior in college now, but Alix says every year he almost flunks out. So far this summer I've seen him with three different girls in his car. He tends to disappear for three or four days at a time and no one knows where he is or what he's doing. He may be a disappointment to Big Phil, but I'll tell you this—if I'm the son every father wishes he had, then Shawn's the son every father wishes he'd been.

"Well, if it isn't my two favorite men."

Big Phil and I turn to see Alix behind us. She's wearing white shorts and a pink polo shirt, and her face, arms, and legs have a slightly reddish cast, like a sun- and windburn over a tan. She gives us both a hug and kiss on the cheek.

"Based on that greeting I'd say you were a second today," Big Phil tells her.

Alix crinkles her sunburned nose. "Third, smarty pants. But it was a real come-from-behind effort and we beat Nancy Marcus's boat."

Phil smiles. He loves the winning spirit. "Hungry?"

"Starved," Alix says. She helps herself to a hamburger and beer, and pulls up a chair. More than anything, Alix loves to be one of The Guys, complete with beer in hand. Maybe that's why she's a prude. The Guys don't make love to each other.

"So, how did it go this afternoon?" she asks, looking out at the trampled lawn.

"Looked pretty good to me," Big Phil says with obvious satisfaction.

Alix turns to me in my greasy plastic apron. "Have a good time?"

"Loved every second of it," I reply, trying to keep a straight face.

Alix hangs around and helps Phil and me clean up. This is surprising, since she will usually disappear at the prospect of undesirable chores. But this evening she stays until the end, sealing garbage bags with twistums, putting away lawn chairs, and picking up odds and ends.

By the time we finish it's getting dark out. Lights are going on inside the house as The Cold One prepares for night. Neither Alix nor I want to hang around, but it's Sunday and most of Alix's night spots are either closed or guaranteed to be dead. Finally she suggests we get lounges and pull them down onto the lawn so that we can watch the harbor as it lights up.

This too is unusual. Normally on a Sunday night Alix would be waiting eagerly for another edition of the Dr. Jo Truth and Sex Radio Hour. Actually, it's the Dr. Joseph Hurbrosky Human Sexuality Clinic, and Alix isn't alone. Probably 90% of the kids between the ages of eleven and nineteen around here listen to him. And a lot of adults too. People call up and discuss their most intimate sexual problems with good old Dr. Jo, and if you listen long enough, you'll hear some pretty incredible stuff. Gordy is a real Dr. Jo addict. Alix is a pretty steady fan too.

But tonight she doesn't seem to be thinking about him as we pull the chaises down onto the lawn. It's dark enough now for the bug zapper in the backyard to go on, emitting its dull blue light and frying any bug that gets too close. Alix and I sit next to each other and I feel her reach over for my hand. It's pretty nice here, feeling the cool evening breeze, watching the lights go on in the harbor, and listening to the bugs crackle and sizzle.

"What are you thinking about?" Alix asks softly.

"Bugs," I reply.

Alix chuckles slightly. "Really?"

"Yeah, but I'm also thinking that it's nice to be out here, looking over the harbor with you." And I mean this sincerely. Dr. Sex and his wild band of hormones appear to have taken the night off.

"Are you having a good summer, Scott?" Alix asks.

"Yeah, so far so good. What about you?"

Alix leans back in her chaise and gazes up at the dark sky. "Oh, I don't know. I guess it's been a little disappointing."

"Why?" I ask.

"Because so many of my friends have gone away. Chris is in Europe. Karla went to South America to visit her uncle. Rachel is sailing with her family in Maine. There's hardly anyone around."

"I'm around," I tell her.

"But all you do is work, Scott," she says, pushing her chestnut hair away from her face. "I'm not blaming you, but I don't have anyone to do anything with most of the time."

"I guess I could cut out a couple of lawn jobs in the morning," I tell her.

"But you still wouldn't be around in the afternoon and evening," she says.

"Isn't there anyone else?" I ask.

"Well, there's Joanne Hawken, whom I can stand for about five minutes at a time before she drives me crazy. And there's my cousin Cindy, who crewed for me today."

"Well, there you go."

"But she's leaving for Nantucket tomorrow for two weeks."

"Oh."

Out in the harbor the boats are coming in from a long Sunday on the water. You can just make out the green and red running lights and you can hear the voices and laughter carrying over the water.

"She invited me to go with her," Alix says.

"Who?"

"Cindy."

"To Nantucket?"

"Uh-huh."

"For two weeks?"

Alix's answer is barely audible, but I know it's an affirmative. She wants to go to Nantucket.

"When would you leave?" I ask.

"Tomorrow."

Talk about short notice. I look up at the stars and try to figure out how I feel about being deserted by my girlfriend for two weeks in the middle of a summer that, to tell you the truth, hasn't been too exciting for me either.

"You're not mad, are you?" Alix asks, squeezing my hand. "I mean, I really hate the idea of leaving you, but it's so boring here. I think I'd go out of my mind if I didn't go away for a while."

I still have not thought of a suitable reply, basically because I'm not sure how I feel about Alix going away. But Alix must think my silence means I'm angry, because she gets up and sits down on the side of my lounge, taking my hand in both of hers, her blue eyes looking so innocently into mine.

"Scott, please try to understand. I don't want to leave you, I really don't. I don't think we've ever been apart for that long before. But I just know that if I don't go I'll be miserable and I'll probably make you miserable too."

Feeling pressed for a response, I nod. But I'm not sure if I'm nodding because I understand or because I agree that if Alix doesn't go away she'll make us both miserable. The weird thing is that I'm not thinking about Alix, I'm thinking about Paula. Her face and her bronzed, bikinied body keep flashing into my mind every time Alix says "two weeks." Those hormones didn't take the night off after all.

I reach up and pull Alix to my chest. She snuggles comfortably against my shoulder and kisses my chin and I press my face into her hair. She smells like sunshine and she's beautiful and she's my girl friend, and suddenly I feel the way I used to feel before we started having fights. Sex just can't be that important, I tell myself. Not when two people care about each other. I was wrong to think that I didn't care for her anymore. I do, and I'll miss her while she's gone.

And I swear I won't think about Paula anymore.

CHAPTER 12

For the first two days that Alix was away I purposely slept late so that I wouldn't have to watch Romeo from Texaco exit Paula's window at breakfast. But on the third morning I'm up early because there are lawns to cut.

Breakfast at the Tauscher residence these days means taking a bite of eggs or toast and then looking out the window to make sure you haven't missed anything. Romeo has become a regular breakfasttime feature, like the news and weather on the radio. But apparently my parents and Kerry still haven't caught on to his schedule yet. At 8:05 I'm the only one who isn't sneaking peeks across the yard.

"Don't bother," I tell them. "He won't be out until eight fifteen."

"He didn't come out at all yesterday," Kerry says.

"Did it ever occur to you that maybe he doesn't spend every night there?" I ask.

My parents look uncomfortable. I guess this isn't exactly the kind of sex education they hoped Kerry would get.

My sister, however, is undaunted. Now she turns to my parents and says, "Do people have intercourse every night?"

I watch while my mother and father toss this invisible hot

potato back and forth with their eyes. Then my mother says,
"Not usually, dear."

And my father adds, "But sometimes."

Now my mother frowns at my father. Meanwhile Kerry scowls
at both of them. Bet I know what she's thinking. How could
they have intercourse? I've wondered about that too. It's not
that they're so old, but my father is pretty flabby and sweaty and
he does have this weird body smell. Not BO, just his natural
smell, if you know what I mean. And while my mother is in
pretty good shape from tennis, she's sort of wrinkly around the
eyes and chin, and she could have two of the ugliest feet ever
stuck on a pair of human legs. I mean, it is hard to imagine those
two actually romping in the sack together. Still, thanks to sex ed,
we know it happens. People in their fifties, sixties, even seventies
do it. But that doesn't mean it isn't gross to think about.

As breakfast continues, Kerry and my mother keep glancing
anxiously out the window. Now, however, they're not watching
for Romeo. Instead, they're looking at the sky. It's getting gray
and windy outside and dark rain clouds have started rolling in.
Green leaves, twigs, even small branches from trees, fly past our
window, and in the kitchen you can feel the sudden change in
the air. There's a summer storm coming.

"Darn." My sister is sulking at the kitchen table with her head
propped up in her hands. Tennis today is a washout. It has
started to rain so hard that you'd think some giant was dumping
huge buckets of water on our house. But Kerry's bad luck is my
good fortune. A rainstorm like this means an unexpected day off
from mowing and parking. Across the table from Kerry, I'm
sitting back with my hands behind my head, trying to decide if I
should go back to bed.

My mother has just gone into the living room where she puts
an old Beatles album on the stereo. She always does that on rainy
days, although none of us knows why. Now she sits down at the
kitchen table again, humming along while the moptops sing
about taxmen and yellow submarines. (My father has already

departed for the office. Neither rain nor snow nor gloom of night shall keep him from his plastic brides and grooms.)

"How about a game of Scrabble?" my mother suggests brightly.

Kerry groans. "Give us a break, Mom."

Another branch of leaves is blown to the ground and I look across at the Finkels'. Romeo from Texaco is standing under the overhang outside the house, smoking a butt and waiting for the rain to let up. With the onset of the storm none of us noticed him leave Paula's bedroom.

"How long do you think he's gonna stand there?" I ask.

Kerry and my mother glance through the window.

"God, he's gross-looking," Kerry says. "How could she have anything to do with him?"

My mother sips her coffee and does not reply. I bet she is thinking that this is only part of the great mystery going on next door.

"How come you never talked to Mrs. Finkel?" I ask.

"I guess I wasn't sure it was any of our business," Mom tells us.

"Even if what Paula's doing is wrong?" Kerry asks.

My mother glances at me uncomfortably. This is a tough question, especially for our mother, who, along with our father, has always stood for what is good and right and just.

"Well, Kerry, it's very difficult to tell other people how to raise their children," my mother tries to explain. "I do feel that what Paula is doing is very wrong and I think that most people, including her mother, would feel that way. But we are not that friendly with Mrs. Finkel and it would be difficult to intrude."

Kerry seems satisfied with that answer and my mother starts to relax. But I've got a question too.

"Why is it so wrong?"

My mother looks at me and rolls her eyes.

"I mean, in some cultures women get married and have babies by the time they're twelve or thirteen," I explain.

"That's true," my mother says. "And in those cultures that is an acceptable form of behavior. But in our culture it isn't."

"But why not?"

"Because in this society it is generally felt that young girls do not have the maturity to understand the implications of what they're doing at that age."

"I thought it was because Paula isn't married," Kerry says.

"Oh, that too," my mother says.

"Hardly anyone waits until they're married these days," I tell Kerry.

My mother frowns. "First of all, that is not true. Some people prefer to wait. And those who don't are usually sure that the person they have relations with is the person they're going to marry."

"Did you wait?" Kerry asks.

"Well, uh, your father and I waited until we were very much in love and we knew we were going to get married."

"In other words, you didn't wait until you were married," I tell her.

Kerry's eyes widen. My mother turns to her.

"To be perfectly honest, we didn't. But we knew we were going to get married."

"Because he'd already asked you, right?" Kerry says.

"Well, I, uh, assume so, but I can't really recall exactly."

Kerry and I glance at each other. Somehow it seems like she would not only remember, but would be able to recite the day, hour and minute, weather conditions and barometric readings. But before we can press our interrogation further, the phone rings and Kerry jumps up to answer it. My mother looks relieved.

Kerry talks for a moment and then turns to her. "Mom, Andrea says there's an indoor court available at the racket club. Will you take us? Please?"

"Oh, all right." My mother turns to me. "And what are you going to do today?"

"Go back to sleep."

An unexpected pleasure—to be lying in bed at ten thirty in the morning, listening to music, knowing that unless it magically dries up outside, I will have the whole day off. No Mrs. Bermans crying about their lawns, no club members screaming that some-one changed the station on their car radios. Ah, it feels great to have nothing to do.

Downstairs the doorbell rings. I pull on a pair of jeans and go down. "Who is it?"

"Paula Finkel."

Paula? I open the door and she's standing outside wearing jeans, a denim jacket with some rock-and-roll buttons on it, and a small black purse over her shoulder. It's still raining and little beads of water hang on her hair. I also notice there are some scratches on her face and her right eye looks black-and-blue. Both eyes are red-rimmed, as if she's been crying.

"Uh, hi," I manage to say.

"Look, I'm sorry to bother you, but could you give me a ride to the train station?" she asks.

I scratch my head, not sure what's going on. "You want to come in?"

Paula shrugs and steps into the house and I close the door behind her.

"Hungry? Want something to eat?" I ask.

She shakes her head. "I want to go to the train station." Her voice is strained and she blinks a couple of times as if she's fighting back tears. I'm still trying to figure out what to do when I hear someone outside shout "Paula! Paula, where are you?"

"Oh, God," Paula gasps, and crouches down behind a chair. "Don't tell her I'm here."

Through the window I see Mrs. Finkel standing on the side-walk in front of our houses, wearing a light blue nightgown and slippers and holding a clear plastic umbrella.

"Paula!" she shouts again. "Paula, where the hell are you?"

Man, this is weird. Now Mrs. Finkel looks toward our house and I also duck out of sight. She stares in our direction for a moment and then walks back up her driveway and into her house.

"Is she gone?" Paula asks from behind the chair.

"Yeah. What's going on?"

"She's a witch," she says, getting up.

"Did she hurt you?" I ask, looking at the marks on her face.

Paula doesn't answer. Come to think of it, it's a fairly stupid question. I mean, unless Paula scratched herself and punched herself in the eye, there aren't many other choices. She gives me a pleading look and I know she wants me to cut out the questions and take her to the train station. I leave her in the hall for a moment and go back upstairs to get my keys and wallet. When I come back downstairs, Paula is standing exactly where I left her. The look on her face is sort of hard and blank, like someone who's seen things they don't want to remember.

"Ready?"

She nods and we go through the kitchen and out into the garage to the van. Paula insists on crouching down in the back while I go down the driveway and out onto the street. As soon as we're away from the house she comes in front with me.

"Phew," she says, waving her hand in front of her nose. "It smells like rotten leaves in here."

"Yeah, I've been meaning to clean it out."

The van backfires a couple of times and accelerates in uneven lurches. Paula puts her hand against the dashboard to steady herself.

"I know it's none of my business," I tell her as we head toward the station, "but if things are really bad at your house, you can get help. I mean, there are places you can go."

"I'm going to the city," she says, staring straight ahead.

"You have a friend there or something?"

She doesn't answer.

We get to the station and Paula gets out without saying thanks. I have a feeling she didn't bother to check the train schedule before she left. She's just going to hang around until the next train comes. I put the van in gear and start to pull away, but then I stop. I don't know. The whole thing just bothers me. Suppose they find her tomorrow morning in some alley with her throat slashed. Or she gets picked up by some pimp and sold into white slavery. Chances are nothing that bad would happen. She'd probably just wander around the city for a couple of hours, spend what money she had, and then come home. Still, it wouldn't make things any better for her.

So maybe I could talk to her. I know it's crazy and it's none of my business, but I park the van and go inside.

CHAPTER 13

It isn't much of a train station, really. Just an old red brick building with some benches inside, and a ticket booth that never seems to be open. There's a little newsstand in one corner where you can buy a paper or a candy bar or a three-day-old Danish. Lots of graffiti on the walls, mostly the names of rock bands. The whole place smells like a soggy cigarette butt.

There's hardly anyone around, just a couple of derelict types probably looking to get out of the rain. Paula's sitting on one of the benches, smoking a cigarette, swinging one leg crossed over the other. I sit down next to her. She doesn't look particularly pleased to see me.

For a while we just sit and watch one of the derelicts cover a bench with old newspapers and then lie down on it for a nap. The other bum is fishing through the garbage can. Where do these guys come from? I wonder. And how do they wind up here? Could they have once had a house in the suburbs and kids and a job?

I notice Paula sneak a peek at me. She probably thinks I want to have a serious conversation about her problems. Come to think of it, that's what I was planning to do, but maybe it's not the right idea. Maybe I'd be better off trying to think of something crazy and fun, something to get her mind off her problems.

"Hey, feel like going fishing?" I ask.

She gives me a look.

"I'm serious. I know a guy who has a boat."

"It's raining," she says.

"So? We'll wear ponchos."

"You're crazy."

"I'm serious. Besides, they say the fish bite the best when it rains."

Paula tries to ignore me.

"Look, what are you gonna do in the city by yourself? Go to a movie? Walk around and get wet? Sit in Grand Central Station and watch the bums there? Come on, we could have some fun."

Paula drops the butt of her cigarette on the floor and crushes it with her foot. "You're really serious."

"Sure I am. This is the first real day off I've had in weeks and I'm not gonna spend it sitting in this railroad station."

Paula sighs and looks up at the ceiling. "God, I can't believe this."

"He probably took the day off and went fishing too."

Paula grins a little. "Would we have to go far?"

"Uh . . . no, just out in the harbor."

She nods. "Okay, but you have to put the worm on my hook."

"It's a deal."

To tell you the truth, I'm sort of surprised I got her to agree.

So we're going fishing. First we go back to my house to pick up gear and ponchos, then to the bait store for a box of sand worms, and finally to the marina, where Albert keeps the *Titanic*. When you get right down to it, it was pretty nice of him to say we could use it. He's a complicated guy. Sometimes he can be a real pain in the butt, and stingy too. Other times he'll be real generous.

Paula and I get everything in the boat and shove off. There's no point in going very far. In this part of the Sound you're going to get the same junk fish wherever you go. Out in the harbor the water is a dull gray-green, like the color of our ponchos. The sky is gray and the rain has changed from a downpour to a drizzle.

There's hardly anyone else out on the water. Just one sailboat and a guy in a dory.

When we start fishing, Paula is like a little kid again. She makes all the right noises: "Ich" when I put the worm on her hook; "Eeek!" when she gets her first bite; and "Oh, gross!" when I pull the hook out of the first eel she catches and crush its skull so it won't steal any more bait.

We don't talk about her mother, or the marks on her face, or Romeo from Texaco. To tell you the truth, we don't talk much at all. We just fish and get rain on our faces and in our sneakers and we watch the terns and sea gulls circle and squawk. Out in the Sound a tanker goes by and a couple of stinkpots crisscross paths. Paula tries to smoke but her cigarettes won't stay lit in the rain. She takes out some gum and offers me a stick. I guess she didn't have time to put on any makeup before she left her house because her face looks plain. After a while she reminds me of any other fifteen-year-old girl having a good time.

By late afternoon we've had a typical harbor day of fishing: a lot of eels, a few blowfish and snappers and two sickly-looking flounders. Nothing worth keeping. It's starting to get colder and windy, and Paula shivers a little, so we go in. Back at the marina she goes off to use the bathroom while I stay behind at the boat to wash away the eel slime and worm blood with a hose.

Paula takes a long time in the bathroom and when she comes out, I see why. She's put on all this makeup. I have mixed feelings about that. While we were out in the boat it occurred to me that I was sort of treating her like my little sister. The thing is, Kerry and I have never done much together. It's not that we don't like each other, it's just that we don't have the same interests. This may sound weird, but when Paula and I were fishing, I kind of felt like I was making up for not being such a hot brother to my own sister.

Anyway, with all that makeup on, it's hard for me to think of Paula as my sister. I also notice that she's left a couple of buttons on her blouse open. Those hormones are starting to heat up again.

Since neither Paula nor I had any lunch, we go to Cook's. It's a big sprawling place on the Post Road that kind of looks like a school cafeteria on the inside, only with better food and a whole room full of the latest video games.

Cook's is pretty empty this afternoon, just a bunch of kids by the video games and a couple of mother-types sitting around one of the tables drinking coffee.

I get a burger, fries, and a lime rickey and buy Paula the vanilla ice cream cone with sprinkles I owe her from our swimming race. We sit down at one of the tables near the windows.

"Tell me about your girlfriend," Paula says between licks of her cone.

The question surprises me. I haven't thought about Alix all day.

"What about her?"

"Do you like her a lot?"

"I guess." Sneaky answer.

"How come you're not with her today?" Paula asks.

"She went away to visit friends."

"What's she like?"

"Aw, I don't know. I guess she's smart and pretty."

"Do you think you'll marry her?"

Not if The Cold One has any say. "I don't know. I gotta finish high school and go to college. I think marriage is pretty far away."

"I'm going to marry Eddie," she says.

"Who?"

"My boyfriend."

"The guy who works at the Texaco station?"

Paula looks surprised. "How'd you know that?"

"I see him crawl out of your window in the morning."

The next thing I know, the ice cream cone falls out of her hand and hits the tabletop with a splat. Paula quickly picks it up again and wipes the table with some napkins. Then she stares silently at me while I wonder why I told her. I really don't know why. Then again, if I really thought about it, I probably wouldn't understand half the things I've done with her.

"Do your parents know?" she asks.

"They've seen him."

"Oh, God." She actually looks sick. "You think they'd tell my mother?"

"They seem to feel that it's none of their business."

Paula nods and gets up to throw her ice cream cone away. I guess she just lost her appetite.

"That would be the end if she ever found out," she says, sitting down again. "You won't tell anyone?"

I shake my head.

Talk about uncomfortable silences. Paula and I sit there while I pick at a couple of fries that have become soggy with catsup. I know what she's thinking: I know this deep, dark secret about her. Maybe she feels like it gives me an advantage. Puts her at my mercy or something.

After a few more moments of silence Paula starts to get up again. "Uh, listen, do you think you could take me home? My mother'll probably call the cops if I don't come back soon."

Before I can answer, she starts walking toward the exit.

Why did I do it? I swear I don't know. What she does with Eddie from Texaco really isn't any of my business and I probably should have kept my mouth closed. The weird thing is, in a way I'm kind of glad I said it.

CHAPTER 14

Uh-oh. There's a big greasy black spot on the garage floor where I normally park the van. I go inside to get a flashlight and then get down on the floor and slide under my baby. Just as I feared: Shiny black drops of oil hang from the bottom of the engine block. My van, my baby, is leaking.

Actually it doesn't surprise me much, considering the fact that the van is older than I am. The bottoms of the side panels have completely rusted out; the floor on the passenger side has a big hole covered with plywood; and the mounts for both front and back bumpers have rusted away—hence, no bumpers. The odometer currently reads 41,289.6 miles. My best guess is that it's already rolled over twice, so it's really 241,289.6. A quarter of a million miles. I've only put on the last 867. The guy I bought it from said he had it for four years and the guy before him had it for two. Who knows who owned it before that.

But this is sad. My first car is dying. Even though it's a hunk of junk and even though I'm saving to buy a better car (one The Cold One won't object to having parked in her carport), I never really thought I'd get rid of this one. I figured I'd store it or have it bronzed or something. Show it to my grandchildren someday.

While I'm under the van I hear the door from the kitchen open and close. It must be Kerry. "Scott?"

"Over here."

Footsteps. Then, "What are you doing under your van?"

"Trying to fix it."

"You don't know anything about fixing cars."

"That's beside the point. I like to pretend."

"Do you even know what's wrong with it?"

"Yeah, it's bleeding."

"God, you are strange."

"Look, did you come out here for a reason, or just to bug me?" I ask from beneath the van.

"Did you just drop Paula off at her house?"

"Maybe." (One of my more brilliant replies.)

"Did you spend the day with her?"

"Look, it's none of your business, and the answer is no anyway. I just ran into her at the store and gave her a lift home. I spent the day with Gordy."

"That's funny. Gordy called about an hour ago and wanted to know where you were."

"Oh. Well, maybe I spent the day with Albert."

"No, you didn't. You spent it with Paula while Alix is in Nantucket."

Have you ever tried to have a conversation with someone from under a car? I slide out and look up at my sister.

"I'm going to ask you a favor, Kerry," I tell her, still lying on my back on the garage floor. "A truly huge favor that I swear I'll pay back someday. I'm going to ask you to forget what you just saw and what you just said, okay?"

"Only if you answer one question," Kerry says.

"What?"

"Did you have intercourse with her?"

I stare up at her. "Do you have any idea how infinitely dumb that question is?"

Kerry puts her hands on her hips. "Why else would you have anything to do with her, Scott?"

I get up, dust off my clothes, and switch off the flashlight. Actually, Kerry's question isn't so dumb, all things considered. All I can do is try to explain to her that Paula's not really such a bad kid considering how crapped up her family life is. And how I just thought maybe I could help her out by spending some time with her.

This results in what I can only call an extremely skeptical look on Kerry's face. "Well, you better watch out for her boyfriend. He doesn't look like the understanding type to me." Then she turns and leaves the garage. She may be young, but she is not naive.

After dinner I call Gordy and we decide to go to a movie. As I drive toward his house I begin to think about what Kerry said about Eddie from Texaco. What kind of guy is he? I mean, I know he's a greaser. But then what? A smart greaser? Dumb greaser? Tough greaser? Does he really care about Paula or is he just looking for easy sex?

Then I get an idea. Why not stop by and see? It's on the way to Gordy's anyway.

A few minutes later I park near the garage office. The Texaco is one of these ancient, dimly lit places with a permanent layer of black grime over everything. You get the feeling it's been around since the days when attendants washed your windshield, cleaned your ashtray, and checked your tire pressure without being asked.

Inside I can see Eddie and another guy lounging around. Eddie is sitting behind this messy desk with his boots crossed over each other. He's wearing dirty jeans and an olive-green uniform shirt with the sleeves ripped off. The other guy looks like a smaller version of the same. Maybe these guys aren't born, maybe they're just cloned from each other in a laboratory somewhere.

I step into the office. It's dirty and dim and smells of oil and cigarette smoke. Eddie's buddy has something cupped in his hand, but after he checks me out he reveals it—a newly lit joint. These guys are too much.

"Can you take a look at my van?" I ask.

Eddie and Eddie II don't budge. I get the feeling they're not into unnecessary motion.

"What's the problem?" Eddie asks after he takes a toke off the joint Eddie II has passed to him.

"It's leaking oil."

The two Eddies glance at each other. Then the original Eddie says, "The boss'll have to look at it. He knows those engines."

"Is he around?"

"Naw, come back tomorrow."

"You sure you can't take a look at it?" I ask.

The Eddie brothers shake their heads. You can see these guys are definitely not into work. Why should they be? The boss isn't here and they'll collect the same pay tonight whether they look at the van or just sit around smoking dope.

I'm turning to leave when Eddie II says, "Hey, don't you go with that chick with the red sports car?"

"Which one's that?" Eddie asks his clone.

"The red Mercedes convertible. Her old man is Shuman, the one that owns those dealerships. She always pays with her old man's credit card. A real fox. You know the one."

Eddie nods and glances at me. "Real piece of tail."

"I'll tell her you said so."

Eddie II chuckles and points at my van outside. "How come you drive that wreck?"

I can only shrug. "Know anyone who's giving away free cars?"

Eddie II looks surprised. "I figured with her old man and everything . . ."

I shake my head. Can he really think that Big Phil would give me a new car just because I date his daughter? I start to leave again, but then I have a thought. Looking at Eddie, I say, "Don't you go with that Finkel girl?"

The mood in the office suddenly changes. There's a long pause while Eddie scowls. "How'd you know that?"

"I guess I must have seen you around somewhere."

"Where?" Eddie wants to know. And he doesn't seem too pleased either. His attitude is starting to make me a little uneasy.

"I don't know. Somewhere."

"I thought you said you don't take her anyplace," Eddie II says.

Eddie doesn't answer him. He just stares at me, looking ticked. I definitely have the feeling I said the wrong thing.

"Well, uh, guess I better go," I tell them, inching slowly toward the door.

"Hey," says Eddie.

"Yes?" I'm ready to sprint for the van if things get ugly.

"I don't know no girl named Finkel. You must be thinking about someone else."

"Yeah, sure." I turn and leave, just glad to get out of that office and back into the van. And Paula thinks she's going to marry that guy?

CHAPTER 15

I haven't seen or spoken to Paula since we went fishing. I guess I really spooked her when I said I knew about Eddie. Maybe it's all for the best. Temptation is gone from my life. Now I can stay pure for Alix. Ha, ha.

Tonight I'm back at Cook's again, only this time I'm with the guys. The parking lot at the club emptied out early and we've come over here to grab some food and decide which one of us will get to go to the pool party Sunday night.

I pick up a double cheeseburger, fries, and a chocolate shake and go join the guys.

"Don't they feed you at home?" Albert asks as I put my tray down on the table.

"My mother's on the warpath," I tell them. "No more red meat and nothing fried. I'd starve without this place."

"Yeah, my mother went through that," Gordy says. "Until her boyfriend moved in. Now at least there's hot dogs and bacon again. Even if I do hate smooth peanut butter and butter pecan ice cream."

"He moved in?" Stu asks.

Gordy nods. "Don't ask. It's too depressing. Every day I wish the guy would get hit by a truck or something."

Stu frowns. It's not like Gordy to say things like that.

Albert takes a bite from a slice of pizza. "Hey," he says with his mouth full. "Remember that girl with the white speedboat? The one who nearly sank us? I think I know which marina she keeps it in. I'm gonna go over there tomorrow morning before work. Anyone want to come?"

Gordy and Stu and I look at each other. None of us is particularly interested in another morning of beer and sunstroke on the open seas.

"What are you going to do if you find her?" Gordy asks.

"Well, I figure I can do one of two things," Albert says with a sly grin. "Either I get a date with her or I put a lead fishing weight through her windshield."

"That's what I like about you, Albert," Gordy says. "You're such a rational guy."

"Yeah? Well, at least I'm not an overgrown embryo like you."

"What about the party, Stu?" I ask. A couple of times each summer the club throws a pool party for the "junior members." It's a bad night to park cars because the kids don't tip, but it's a great night to have off because you can get into the party and have a good time.

"One guy gets to go," Stu says. "The others have to work."

"It's my turn," Gordy says.

"What do you mean, it's your turn?" Albert asks.

"I mean, you guys have all gone to the pool party before and I never have," Gordy tells him. "Besides, I deserve to go because I'm having such a crappy summer."

"I think the guy most likely to score should go," Albert says. "If you go, it'll just be a waste."

"Will not."

"Oh, yeah?" Albert says. "Suppose you were at the party and you saw some girl you wanted to meet. What would you do?"

"I'd go up and ask what her name is," Gordy says.

"You see?" Albert says triumphantly. "That's the dumbest line in the world. She'd probably laugh in your face."

"It beats asking her if she wants to see my appendectomy scar," Gordy says.

Stu and I laugh. Albert glares at us. "I was just experimenting, that's all. It's important to be original, you know."

"You're original, all right," Gordy tells him.

Albert lifts his arm as if he's going to slam him. "Aw, shut up."

Stu gets up, goes over to the cashier, and gets some toothpicks. When he comes back he breaks one in half and mixes it up in his hand with the three long ones. "Pick one," he says, holding up his fist with the four toothpicks sticking out of it.

"I never pick the right one," Gordy gripes. "My luck stinks. It's not fair."

"Shut up and pick a toothpick," Albert says as he reaches toward Stu's hand.

I reach for one too. Mine comes up long. So does Gordy's. Albert's got the short one.

"All right, man!" he shouts. "Pool party, here I come."

"It's not fair," Gordy whines again.

"You wouldn't know what to do with a girl if she fell into your lap," Albert says.

"You wanna bet?" Gordy asks angrily.

"Okay, cut it out," Stu says. "Albert drew the short one, so he goes."

Albert and Gordy quiet down and we all get into some serious eating. But as we eat I notice that Gordy keeps looking past Albert and me. We turn around. A few tables over from us, Paula is sitting with some greaser girl. When she sees me, she waves. I wave back and turn to my half-finished burger and fries.

"Who's that?" Gordy asks. "She keeps looking over here."

"Just someone I know," I tell him and take a bite out of my burger. Next to me Albert takes a sip of soda and says, "Hey, Scott, the guy at the marina office told me you used the boat the other day."

Suddenly I lose interest in my food.

"He said you took a girl out fishing," Albert continues. "I thought he must have been mistaken because Alix is up in Nantucket."

Gordy is starting to grin. Even Stu looks interested. Albert's playing this for everything it's worth. He turns to Gordy and Stu. "See that girl over there? The one Scott says is just someone he knows? Well, what he didn't tell you is that she's his next-door neighbor."

"The one who sleeps with that guy from Texaco?" Gordy asks.

Albert grins. "The one who does everything Alix won't do," he says, nudging me in the ribs with his elbow. "And I'm pretty sure she's the one he took out in the boat. Isn't it funny how as soon as Alix goes away Scott takes her fishing? And now she's waving at him in Cook's."

"Albert, you're so far off the mark that it isn't even funny," I tell him.

"Then, what's the story?" Gordy asks.

"There is no story. She's just my next-door neighbor, that's all."

"And what about fishing?" he asks.

"So we went fishing, big deal. What do you think, Albert? That we did it in the boat?"

Gordy and Albert look at each other and grin. I have a feeling I'm overreacting. Unfortunately, that only makes me look more guilty. To make things worse, Paula picks that moment to get up and come over and say hello. She's wearing tight black jeans, a tight pink T-shirt, and a lot of makeup. Albert and Gordy ogle her like crazy.

"Hi, Scott," she says, ignoring, or possibly even enjoying, their glances.

"Uh, hi," I answer, and look back down at my hamburger. Paula waits for me to say something more, but I don't want to give the guys the idea that we're real chummy or anything.

Finally Albert gives me a sharp elbow in the ribs. "You gonna introduce us or what?"

"Uh, Paula Finkel, these are the jerks, oops, I mean guys I work with. Stu Chock, Albert Kantana, and Gordy Price."

"Hi," Paula says.

Albert and Gordy continue to drool at her. It really makes me uncomfortable.

"Well, uh, good seeing you again, Paula," I say. Paula frowns.

I know it must seem like I'm trying to get rid of her, but I'm really just trying to protect her from my horny friends. More than anything I don't want to wake up one morning to find Albert or Gordy crawling out of her window. But Paula can't know I'm thinking that. She walks away without saying good-bye.

"Why'd you do that?" Gordy asks.

"Because I didn't want any of you sex maniacs getting ideas."

"Why not?" Albert asks. "Saving her for yourself?"

I can feel my fists clench under the table. Albert is such an expert at twisting things around. Sometimes I just feel like belting him.

CHAPTER 16

Later Stu offers to drive me and Gordy home. I had to leave the van at the Texaco so that Eddie's boss could check it out. Gordy doesn't own a car and sometimes can't get one of his parents'.

I get in front and Gordy gets in back with this big stuffed panda Stu keeps buckled into one of the seats. He won it at Playland one night after sinking about 150 foul shots at one of those sideshow games, and just for the hell of it he stuck it in the backseat. It's been there so long that people don't even blink when they see Stu riding around with this big stuffed bear in his car.

As we drive home Gordy starts acting weird again. He's making slobbering noises. I turn around and see that he's embracing the panda.

"Oh, *ma chérie*," he croons into the bear's furry ear. "Geeve us a leetle keess."

"You stoned or something?" I ask.

"Don't you think she's attractive?" Gordy asks, still hugging the bear.

Stu glances at him in the rearview. "Don't slobber all over it, Gordy."

Gordy lets go of the panda. "She isn't my type anyway."

Stu turns into Gordy's community. It's late and the houses are dark and the streets are quiet. It's almost a full moon tonight and the moonlight bathes everything in a dull glow.

"Sometimes I come through here late at night after work," Gordy says from the back, "and I pass all these houses with the lights out, and I think, someone in one of these houses is doing it. Who knows? Maybe dozens of people are doing it right now. All around us it's happening. All day long it's happening somewhere to someone. It must be happening. These people are married. They have children. They couldn't have children if they didn't do it. It's perfectly natural. The human species would cease to exist if they didn't do it. It's happening all around us. *But it never happens to me!*"

"I changed my mind," Stu says. "You can take the panda home tonight if you want."

"I don't want a panda," Gordy groans. "I don't want to look at naked women in dirty magazines. I want a girl. A real live girl. Flesh and blood. I want someone with body temperature."

"You sound desperate, Gordy," I tell him.

"I am desperate."

"Don't you think you should wait until you're married?" Stu asks, joking.

"Are you kidding?" Gordy gasps. "I might die before that. I could die tomorrow, a virgin. What a miserable waste of a life that would be. 'Here lies Gordon Price, who died at the age of seventeen, a virgin.'"

"You'd go to heaven, Gordy," I tell him as Stu pulls into the Prices' driveway.

"No way," Gordy says. "If impure thoughts were pennies, I'd be a multimillionaire. I'd get sent to hell just because of the stuff I thought when I was ten. There must be something wrong with me."

Stu turns around. "Hey, seriously, Gordy. You like to listen to Dr. Jo, right? Did you ever think about calling him yourself?"

"Yeah, but I work Sunday nights, remember?"

Stu glances at me. I know what he's thinking. "I could fill in for you Sunday night," I tell him.

"This Sunday's the pool party," Gordy says. "We're all working anyway."

"Then next Sunday maybe," Stu tells him.

"Sure," Gordy says, reaching for the car door. "If I haven't ended it all by then."

He gets out and slams the door and Stu backs the Cordoba out of the driveway. "And you think you have it bad," he says as we head toward my house.

I hate to say it, but now that Gordy's not here to distract me I start to feel pretty bummed out myself. Paula Finkel lives in a world where everyone treats her like dirt and now I'm part of that world because of what I did tonight at Cook's. It wasn't her fault and she didn't deserve it. She was just trying to be friendly.

"Stu, you know that girl who came over to the table tonight?"

Stu nods. He's leaning so far forward that his chin is practically resting on the steering wheel. But that's just the way he drives late at night.

"You don't really think I'm fooling around with her, do you?"

"If you tell me you're not, I believe you."

"Her mother's a drunk," I tell him. "She hits her. Her boyfriend uses her for sex, and everyone else thinks she's a slut. But I've kind of gotten to know her and she's not such a bad kid."

Stu nods. I look at him leaning on the steering wheel of the Cordoba like he's got bad sight or something. I know the thing I really want to ask him.

"This may sound dumb, but how old were you the first time?"

"Fourteen."

"How old was the girl?" I ask.

"Uh, sixteen."

I stare out the window, thinking, here I am, seventeen years old. Three years behind.

Stu must know what I'm thinking because he says, "It's not a race, Scott. There are no winners or losers. You just wait until the time is right." He pauses and smiles to himself. "You'll know your golden opportunity when you see it."

I shrug. "I just wish it would happen already."

"You think it's worth giving Alix up for?" he asks.

I look at him. "What do you think of her, Stu?"

"It doesn't matter what I think of her. It matters what you think of her."

I slump down in the seat and put my feet up on the dashboard. "I don't know what I think anymore. She's been away almost a week, and you know what? I miss her, but I don't miss her much. I never realized how tense I feel when I'm with her. I mean, this whole sex thing. When she isn't here, I don't have to think about whether she will or she won't. It's crazy. She went away, but I'm the one who feels like I'm on vacation."

Stu doesn't respond, and in the silence I'm a little amazed at what I've just said. Until the words came out of my mouth, I never realized that they were true. But they are. It's a relief not to have Alix around, and not to have to deal with The Cold One, and not to have to be the substitute son for Big Phil. And I don't think it has anything to do with Paula either.

We pull into my driveway. The moonlight almost makes it seem like late afternoon instead of after midnight. Stu stares up through the windshield at the sky. "Hey, Scott, think you could lend me twenty until Friday?"

I reach for my wallet. "Got a date tonight?"

Stu chuckles. "Yeah."

I hand him two tens and get out of the car. Stu waves and backs slowly down the driveway. He's borrowed money from me before and he's always been good for it. I feel a little envious. Imagine going out on a date at midnight.

CHAPTER 17

Another sleepless night. The moonlight is so bright that I have to close the shades in my room to keep it out. I'm lying in bed still feeling bad about the way I treated Paula at Cook's. And I wish I hadn't asked Stu how old he was the first time. Fourteen. Maybe it's not a race, but here I am, seventeen and still no golden opportunity in sight. Except Paula. Hey, jerk, I tell myself, don't think about that.

But the most depressing thing about tonight wasn't Paula or Stu. It was Gordy. Seeing him act so berserk about sex just reminded me of myself. Just because he can't keep quiet about it and I can doesn't make us any different. I know exactly how he feels. It's like dying of thirst in the middle of a huge lake filled with sparkling fresh water. We're surrounded by it, Gordy and me. But we can't touch it.

Alix says all I have on my mind is sex. How can you avoid it? You walk up to a newsstand to get a candy bar and dozens of beautiful seminaked women stare at you from the covers of magazines. And they're not all sex magazines either. Some of the prettiest, sexiest women are on magazines for women. You turn on the radio and hear this sexy, seductive voice inviting you to some dance club and it's not too subtly implied that if you go you'll meet other girls with sultry, sexy voices. And forget the movies. I can't remember the last time there was a movie about teenagers that wasn't R-rated.

I turn over on my stomach and then on my side, but it's no use. I can't stop thinking about it. Even my parents aren't immune. My father has this one drawer where he keeps old shirts he hardly wears anymore and underneath them are two magazines that make *Penthouse* look like the *Reader's Digest.* I don't even know where you can get magazines like that. And my mother? Well, I once overheard her talking on the telephone to a friend and saying that one of the reasons she liked calling lines at major tournaments was that she got so close to those sexy young tennis stars in their skimpy little shorts.

So I'm not the only one with sex on the brain. Only it's like acne—at certain times of your life you have more of it than at other times. And teenagers get it bad. If girls don't want guys to think about it, why do they wear such skimpy bathing suits to the beach? And such tight clothes to school? I remember Alix and I once had an argument after we saw a TV show about topless bathing. Alix said when a woman goes topless at the beach she's not being a tease, she's being natural. Well, I'm natural too. And part of being natural is having a natural sex drive. A man reaches the peak of his sexuality in his late teens and early twenties. The peak of frustration too.

My eyes are wide open. There's no sense in lying here in bed. I'm not gonna fall asleep. I get up and go out into the hall in the dark and down the stairs. The steps creak as I go down, but I doubt it will bother anyone. We all get up once in a while and go down to the kitchen when we're thirsty or hungry and can't sleep.

But I'm not hungry or thirsty, and I find myself sitting in my underwear at the kitchen table in the dark, staring across the yard at Paula's window. There's a light on inside, but the curtain is closed. What are they doing? I'm so curious that I almost want to go outside and sneak up to the window and see if I can look in.

After a while the light goes out in Paula's window, but I still don't move. A little while later I hear footsteps coming down the stairs. The sound of flopping slippers. It's my mother.

"Scott?" she whispers into the kitchen. "Are you in here?"

"Yeah. Don't turn on the light, okay?" I whisper back. It's not that I don't want her to see me in my underwear, it's just that I hate the glare of bright lights after my eyes have gotten used to the dark.

My mother's wearing a long pink nightgown and she looks like a ghost as she walks in the dark.

"Is anything wrong?" she asks.

"No."

"You just happen to be sitting in the kitchen in the dark in the middle of the night for fun?"

"I'm dealing with adolescent turmoil."

My mother sits down at the kitchen table with me. In the moonlight her face looks long and pale.

"You miss Alix? It must be difficult when she's away."

I only gaze at her in the grayish light. Where does she get these ideas from? She must have this fantasy that I have this wonderful mature relationship with Alix. To her it's like some kind of fairy tale romance, a happy little soap opera she gets to enjoy vicariously. I wonder what she'd say if I told her the reason I can't sleep tonight is because I'm being tormented by sexual temptation and confusion.

"Is there any way I can help?" she asks.

"Thanks, Mom," I tell her. "But I think this is something I'll just have to deal with by myself."

I guess I wish she'd go back upstairs and leave me alone, but she stays sitting with me in the dark. The only illumination in the room comes through the window in the form of moonlight and from the wall clock over the refrigerator. The only sounds are the whir of the clock's electric gears and the grumble of the refrigerator as it struggles in the summer heat.

"When you were younger, you always used to talk to me," my mother says with a hint of sadness in her voice.

"It's different now, Mom."

In the dark my mother nods. "I know. It's just hard to believe how much you've grown up."

It makes me feel bad to hear her talk like that. Usually she's a pretty feisty lady. If she isn't rushing off to the tennis courts, then she's nagging Kerry or me to clean our rooms, or she's angry at the maid for not doing a good job in the bathroom, or she's on the phone laughing hysterically with one of her friends. I'm used to all those moods. I can deal with them. But to hear her sound so glum, it's just not like her.

"A year from now you'll be going away to college and I'll be forty years old," she says wistfully. "Do you know what's so strange, Scott? They still play the songs on the radio that we used to listen to when I was in college."

"The Beatles?"

In the dark my mother nods. I think she's smiling now. "Yes, the Beatles."

Well, that's cute, I think to myself.

"Scott, do you have any idea where you were conceived?"

I'm not exactly sure what she means by that. "You mean, where I was born?"

"No, dear, you were born in New York Hospital. I meant, where you were conceived. The night you were actually created."

I don't know how to answer that. Do I really want to know the history of my mother's sex life?

"Did you ever hear of Woodstock?" she asks.

"Sure, it's a town in upstate New York."

"But, you know it was also a huge rock festival during the summer of 1969."

"Yeah, I saw that movie on TV."

"Your father and I were there, Scott."

"At the festival?"

My mother looks out at the moon and nods. Is this a joke? My mother and father went to a rock festival?

"I'll never forget it," she says, still gazing outside. "It was our first summer out of college and we were both living in Greenwich Village. Your father was selling toys for the Educational

Toy Company and I was a salesgirl at Bloomingdale's. The summer weekends in the city were so hot that we'd do practically anything to get away.

"Well, your father had a friend from college, a real crazy man named Doug who lived on a farm upstate. He'd been a business major in college but then he'd become a hippie. He had a long blond beard and a blond ponytail that went down to the middle of his back. He grew his own food and his own pot and every time we went to see him he'd try to get us to take LSD or some other crazy drug."

I lift an eyebrow. My mother knew someone who took LSD? A friend of my father's from college?

My mother continues. "Doug invited us up to his farm for the rock festival. Neither of us really wanted to go, but it was August and so hot that we were desperate to get out of the city. I think we took Friday off and left Thursday night. The first strange thing we noticed was that the farther north we went, the worse the traffic got. Then we heard on the radio that hundreds of thousands of people were going to this festival. I remember your father and I agreeing in the car that we would go to Doug's but not to Woodstock.

"We got to Doug's around ten at night and he insisted that we just go take a look. So we agreed. I'll never forget it. The road was completely jammed with people and cars. Your father kept telling Doug to turn around, but he was intent on seeing what was going on, and to be honest, after a while we became a little curious too. We really had the feeling that something unusual was happening.

"We finally got to the festival grounds around one in the morning and it was the most amazing thing we'd ever seen. Mass confusion. A huge sea of people spread out over a field making fires and pitching tents in the dark, waiting for morning and the festival to begin. Then, of course, Doug said we had to stay. The road out was closed.

"That was the only time I was scared. I thought we'd starve to death or freeze. But Doug had packed the trunk of his car with sleeping bags and food. He knew all along we were going to stay."

"So you stayed for the whole thing, huh?" I ask. It's kind of funny, thinking of my superstraight parents mixed in with half a million stoned-out hippies listening to rock and roll for three days.

"We didn't leave until Monday morning," my mother says. "It wasn't something I'd ever do again. It rained and everything got wet and muddy and there weren't enough toilets and people kept saying that there were bad drugs going around. But everyone we met was wonderful. People shared all the water and food they had. Everyone was remarkably calm and friendly and it really was fun to see all those groups perform."

"But what's it have to do with me?" I ask.

"It's simple. Your father and I spent three nights together in the same sleeping bag and on the third night . . . well, it was really early Sunday morning, but it was still dark and The Who was performing *Tommy.*"

"The rock opera?"

"That's right," my mother says. "You were conceived early Sunday morning while The Who played *Tommy.*"

"You're kidding."

"Nope."

"How do you know?" I ask.

"Mothers know those things," she tells me. "And besides, you were born exactly nine months later to the day."

Outside a car pulls into the Finkels' driveway, then backs out and goes back the way it came. In the kitchen I'm trying to imagine my mother and father in a sleeping bag while The Who played. I don't think they could even fit in the same sleeping bag today.

"Hey, Mom, did Dad have long hair?"

She nods. "And long sideburns too."

It's hard to believe.

"There's something else, Scott."

"What?"

"We weren't married."

For a second I don't get it. "You never got married?"

"Of course we got married. It's just that on the night you were conceived we weren't married."

It still takes me a couple of seconds to figure it out. "Does that mean I'm illegitimate?"

My mother actually laughs out loud. "No, silly, it just means that we got married after you were conceived."

"How come you're telling me now?"

"Because I think you're old enough to understand, and I wanted to be the one to tell you before you heard it from one of your cousins."

"Does Kerry know?"

"No, and I don't want you to tell her. She's not old enough to know yet."

For a few moments we just sit there in the dark. This is a lot to digest all at once. That I, humble valet parker and gardener, was conceived in a sleeping bag while The Who played *Tommy* at history's most famous rock and roll festival. By parents who weren't married at the time.

My mother yawns and gets up. "I have to go back to bed. Kerry has a tournament in Port Washington early in the morning."

She starts to leave, but I have one more question. "Mom, you and Dad didn't get married just because of me, did you?"

"No, we got married because we wanted to get married."

"You sure?"

"Yes. Now go to bed."

The next morning at breakfast I keep looking over at my father. It's hard to believe that this overweight, balding guy in the brown suit actually went to a rock festival with my mother, slept with her in a sleeping bag, and got her pregnant with me before they were married.

In the middle of his pancakes he looks up at me. "What are you grinning at?"

"Uh . . ." I glance at my mother and then back at him. "Nothing, Pop."

CHAPTER 18

Lawn-cutting time again. As usual, Mrs. Berman is waiting for me in her driveway. She practically has tears running down her cheeks as she points out her lawn's latest problem—brown patches of grass. I kneel down and take a look. Uh-oh. There's no doubt about it. In addition to the slime, the bare spots, and the ugly tree roots, Mrs. Berman's lawn has chinch bugs.

I explain this to Mrs. Berman and she gets this pained "Why me?" look on her face. What can I tell her? Some people are born rich, some are born poor. It's the same with lawns. All I can promise her is that I'll cut the lawn today and come back tomorrow morning to take care of the little buggers.

Next stop, the Finkels'. It's humid and overcast today. Hot, but not torturous. I cut the front and back, but Paula isn't by the pool. As I push the mower past the side of the house where her room is, I stop and tap on her window.

Paula's face appears quickly, but when she sees me, she frowns. The same frown I saw in Cook's. She pushes open the window. "What do you want?"

"I want to apologize for the other night."

"There's nothing to apologize for," she says. But I can tell from her voice that she's hurt.

"Yes, there is," I tell her. "Can you come out? I want to talk to you."

Paula thinks for a moment and then says, "Okay, but not here. I'll meet you at the playground in half an hour."

That gives me time to put the tools of my trade back in the van and park it in our garage. Romeo's boss at Texaco had bad news: My baby needs an engine overhaul. As much as I love her, I'd rather put the money toward a new set of wheels.

Later I'm sitting on a swing in this little playground near our houses. Someone nearby is barbecuing chicken for lunch and the smell wafts toward me, bringing fond memories of when my father used to cook ribs and chicken on our outdoor grill. But barbecued foods have gone the way of red meat, salt, and sugar in our house. My mother read an article that barbecued meats are carcinogenic. Sometimes I think life is carcinogenic.

I push off from the sand and swing back and forth, wondering if I will ever become as insane as the adults around me—developing ulcers over a dumb patch of grass and eliminating everything truly good from my diet because some newspaper article tells me to. It seems so unlikely, and yet I know all these adults were once teenagers too. Some of them went to rock festivals and had sex before they were married. What happened later that made them so weird?

Before I can think about it further I see Paula strolling barefoot down the sidewalk, wearing shorts and a white T-shirt and smoking a cigarette. She hardly looks at me as she sits down on the swing next to mine and gives it a little push.

"Those guys I was with the other night," I tell her. "They're my friends, but a couple of them can be real jerks sometimes."

"The two with the dark hair," Paula says.

"Uh, yeah, how'd you know?"

"I could tell by the way they looked at me."

"I just didn't want them to, you know, get any ideas."

Paula swings back and forth a couple of times. "I can take care of myself."

"Yeah, I know. I'm sorry."

Paula keeps swinging. It's difficult to know what she's thinking because on the swing I can't watch her face.

"You think I'm a tramp, don't you," she says.

It must have taken a lot of guts for her to say that. I can't imagine how to respond.

"God, I hate this," Paula says. "I hate living here. I hate the people here. I hate my mother. I wish I could go away and start all over again somewhere where nobody knew me."

"Like North Carolina?"

"I wish," she says bitterly.

"How come you don't go down there to live?"

"I don't know," she says. "It's something legal. I can go down for vacations, but if I go down when I'm not supposed to, I could get him into a lot of trouble."

She pushes harder and starts swinging higher while I sit motionless on the swing next to her. On the street a new Cadillac with dark-tinted windows passes slowly and then stops. Both Paula and I look at it. I can't see who's inside, but somehow I know they're watching us. The car sits for a moment and then takes off.

"Who was that?" Paula asks.

"Bet you it was someone who knows one of us," I tell her.

Paula starts swinging slower. "What if I told you that I was thinking of breaking up with Eddie?"

"Why?"

"Because he only has one thing on his mind."

That's a laugh. It sounds just like me and Alix. Except for one thing. "I thought you said you were going to marry him."

"Never," Paula says, as firmly as she said a couple of days ago that she was going to. Then she gives me a questioning look. "Do *you* think I should break up with him?"

Do I think she should? Hey, wait a minute. All of a sudden I'm starting to get funny vibes from her. Like the question isn't only what I would think about her breaking up with Eddie, but what would I think about taking Eddie's place? Certain parts of my body start to tingle and buzz. Is this what I've really been after all this time? Is this the golden opportunity?

"I don't know, Paula," I hear myself telling her. "I'm not sure what I think."

Paula kicks some sand with her bare foot. I hope she doesn't think I'm playing hard to get. I really don't know what I want.

"Is Alix still away?" she asks next.

That one catches me by surprise. I'm pretty sure I've never mentioned Alix's name to Paula. That means she must be doing research on her own.

"Yeah, she's gonna be gone until next week."

"Do you miss her?"

I have to admit that Paula isn't very subtle with her questions. "Sort of," I tell her.

"Sort of?" Paula echoes curiously.

"It's hard to explain."

She laughs. "Mr. Mysterious. That's what I'm going to call you," she says. Then she starts into some fairly serious swinging again. What the hell, I might as well join her. Pretty soon we're both heaving and pulling, swinging way up into the air, chains rattling, metal swivels screeching. God, I haven't done this in years. I hold the chains tightly and lean back as I arc downward and then upward again. Then I tuck my legs in and hunch forward as I swing back. Next to me Paula is going almost as high as I am.

"This reminds me," I yell out, "of a kid I used to know named Ricky Guinn. He used to swing as high as he could—maybe seven or eight feet off the ground—and just when the swing reached its highest point, he'd jump off."

"Do it!" Paula yells.

"No way," I yell back.

"Oh, come on."

The next thing I know, I'm seriously considering it. What? Am I out of my mind? Am I nuts? Probably. But all the same, at the top of the next arc, maybe seven feet off the ground, I push off from the seat.

For a split second I hang motionless in the air, and then I fall straight down and hit the sand with a thud. *Whump!* Flat on my back.

"Are you okay?"

I am vaguely aware that Paula slowed down her swing and jumped off. Actually I'm pretty sure I'm okay. Just a little surprised at how hard I hit the sand. And how hard the sand is. A lot harder than it felt when I was eight. I push myself up into a sitting position, and brush the sand off.

"Yeah, I'm okay."

"You were really high when you jumped off," Paula says. "Here." She reaches toward me.

I grab hold of her hands and she leans back as I hoist myself up. But as soon as I'm standing she somehow manages to let herself fall forward into my arms. The next thing I know, her arms are around my waist and her body is pressed against mine. Her chin is resting softly against my chest and she's looking up at me.

"Uh, Paula . . ."

She lets go. "I just wanted to see how it felt," she says with a laugh.

Is it right there in front of me? The golden opportunity? With Paula?

It's funny, but in a way I am getting to like her. It's not romantic or anything. It's just that she manages to be tough and proud in the face of such a crappy situation. Compared to her, Kerry and I have led such soft, protected lives. I couldn't imagine either of our parents getting drunk or hitting us. Our lives are so different from hers that it's hard to believe that we live next door to each other.

But another voice in my head says that's not what we're talking about. What we're talking about is the golden opportunity. Should I or shouldn't I? I don't know. I really don't. My head says no, but those hormones are screaming "Yes! Yes! Yes!" so loud that it feels like everyone around me should be able to hear them too.

CHAPTER 19

Albert stops by the valet shack on the day of the pool party. He has preened himself to preppy *paesano* perfection and stands around rubbing in the fact that while we slave away parking cars tonight he will be chasing girls through the cabanas.

"If I meet any beauties and they have friends, maybe I'll bring 'em down here for you guys," he tells us.

"Don't do us any favors, Albert."

Albert grins. "Hey, I'm only trying to share the wealth."

The rest of us groan. Gordy seems particularly depressed today. "So once again Albert gets to meet the girls while the rest of us go home and play with ourselves," he moans. "You think it's unhealthy to play with yourself too much?"

"Lighten up, Gordy."

"I'm serious, guys."

"We know you're serious. That's your problem."

"Come on, guys, there's no one else I can ask," Gordy says.

"Ask Dr. Jo," says Albert.

Gordy shrugs. "I'd kind of like to, but I don't know. I think I'd feel like an idiot if anyone I knew heard me. I'm just so bummed out. I really don't know what to do. I swear, half the time I feel like ending it all."

Stu looks up. "Maybe you should call Dr. Jo tonight."

"How can I?" Gordy asks. "I gotta work."

"Take the night off," Stu tells him.

"Hey, Stu," I interrupt. "How're we gonna handle the pool party with just two guys?"

"I'll get one of the part-timers to come in," Stu says. He turns to Gordy. "You just try to get through to Dr. Jo, okay?"

Gordy nods solemnly. "Uh, okay, sure. Thanks, Stu, you're a good guy."

The pool party is supposed to be for members only, but it's pretty high up on the summer's list of good parties to crash. One of my jobs as a valet parker is to make sure that only members' cars come into the club. But if a member wants to lend his car to a friend for the night, or if he wants to bring in a whole carload of guests, there's really nothing I can do about it.

With Albert going to the party and Gordy trying to call Dr. Jo, things are really hopping around the valet shack tonight. Stu called in a part-timer named Bobby, who's helping out, but we're still running like crazy. We've got a radio to listen to the Dr. Jo show later when Gordy calls, but in the meantime it's subservience city. Almost all of the cars coming in are filled with kids. It's pretty bad. Not just because they don't tip, but because you feel like a jerk opening the door for some kid who may even be younger than you.

The cars keep streaming in. There's a loud band by the pool and at the valet shack we can hear the noise and the chatter as hundreds of kids try to make themselves heard above the music. So far we've only had to turn away a couple of cars filled with crashers. Most of them will just park out on the road and try to sneak in anyway.

I've just parked a car down in the lot and I'm jogging back when I see Stu leaning over the driver's window of an old blue Ford Pinto. I don't recognize the car, but from its condition I would guess that it's a bunch of crashers and Stu's telling them to get lost. But as I cut in front of the car on my way to the valet shack, I hear someone yell "Scott!"

It's Paula, in the passenger seat of the Pinto, and she's waving at me. I look more closely and see that the driver of the car is the greaser girl who was with her in Cook's. That's a joke. She can't possibly be old enough to have a license.

I lean in the window. "Where'd you steal this thing?"

"It's Christine's brother's car," Paula explains. "He lent it to us for the night."

I bend down a little farther and look across at Christine. She gives me a little smile.

"Hey, Christine," I say, "did your brother lend you his license too?"

Christine stops smiling.

"Look," Stu says as he leans in from the other side. "We can't let you in."

Paula looks up at me. "Please, Scott?"

All I can do is shrug. "It's against the rules."

"Is there anyplace else we can park and get in?" Paula asks.

Stu and I glance across the roof at each other. I should really tell her to get lost, but I can't. "Okay, listen, go back out to the road and down another hundred yards and you'll see a little driveway with a sign that says Service Entrance. Park your car in there. Everyone will think it's just the extra help for the party. Then go into the kitchen and ask for Juan. Tell him you're a friend of mine and I said he should let you into the party. He's a good guy. Don't worry."

Paula gives me a big smile. "Thanks, Scott."

Christine turns the Pinto around and they go out toward the road.

"I didn't think you were such a softy," Stu says.

"Neither did I," I tell him.

By nine thirty there isn't much to do. Everyone who is going to this party has already arrived and no one has left yet. The sounds of loud music, laughter, shouting, and screams (a lot of people get thrown in the pool) bombard us from the other side of the clubhouse. But around the valet shack itself things are quiet. Bobby the part-timer has gone to sneak a peek at the

party. Stu is stretched out on the bench next to me, while I try
to get some tunes on the radio.

"What do you think about Gordy?" Stu asks while I turn the
radio dial.

"He's definitely acting weird," I tell him. "But I never heard
of anyone committing suicide because they couldn't find a girlfriend."

Stu pulls a long splinter out of the bench and uses it to pick
his teeth. "My father committed suicide."

Talk about coming straight out of nowhere. "Really, Stu?"

He nods. "About ten years ago. We never figured out why. He
never acted like anything was wrong. But then one day I came
home from school and he was hanging from the jungle gym in
the backyard."

"You found him?"

"Yeah."

"And you never had the slightest hint?"

Stu shakes his head. "He wasn't the type who let you know
what he was feeling."

Sort of like you, Stu, I can't help thinking.

Just before the Dr. Jo Truth and Sex Radio Hour is about to
begin, we get an unexpected visitor down at the valet shack. It's
Albert and he doesn't look happy.

"Hi, guys," he says, slumping down on the bench and lighting
a Marlboro.

"What are you doing here?" I ask.

"I want to see if Gordy gets to talk to Dr. Jo," he says.

Neither Stu nor I believes him.

"Since when do you care about Gordy getting on the show?" I
ask.

"And what happened to the party?" asks Stu.

Albert takes a deep drag of his cigarette and shrugs. "Big deal.
I don't know. Some people are real jerks."

"Tell us what happened, Albert," Stu says.

"Nothing happened."

"Come off it, Albert," I tell him.

"Well, maybe something happened."

"Like what?"

"Well, like I'm hangin' around near the band and I meet this girl, Angelica. She's somebody's friend from Connecticut or someplace and she's the best-looking chick I've seen since I don't know when, right? So I really get to work. The goal for the night is to get her phone number, address, and a date. I mean, if I could get her behind the cabanas, I wasn't gonna complain. But I was ready to settle for a phone number and a date. This was serious business."

"It must have been for you to settle for just that," I tell him.

Albert shrugs. "So I give her the deluxe treatment. She wants something to drink, I go get it for her. She wants something to eat. No problem, Albert's on his way. And things were working out pretty good, right? We were dancing and having a good time and laughing it up. Things were going so well that I was beginning to think that maybe I would suggest we take a walk behind the cabanas, after all."

He pauses.

"Then what?" I ask.

"You didn't mention your appendectomy scar, did you?" asks Stu.

"No, man, I didn't mention anything," Albert says. "It was her. Her and the stupid four questions."

"What?" I ask.

"You know, the four questions every girl asks as soon as things start to get a little serious. How old are you? Where do you live? Do you have a car? And what school do you go to?"

"So?" says Stu.

"I tell you, man," Albert says. "I know what girls like Angelica want. They want an older guy who goes to college. They don't want some punk high school kid. So I told her I went to Harvard."

Stu starts chuckling and Albert glares at him. "Yeah, funny, Stu. So it turns out her brother goes to Harvard. And the next thing I know she's asking me do I know her brother and do I know this one and that one and did I ever hang out here and did

I ever eat there. I mean, she even asks me about this stupid professor her brother has. So what am I supposed to do, make all that crap up?"

"Try a community college next time," I tell him.

Albert shakes his head. "So I told her I had to use the bathroom, and split. I just blew it, guys. And I liked her too."

"Go back and tell her the truth," Stu says.

"Come off it, Stu," Albert says.

"Then go back and meet someone else," I tell him.

But Albert just shrugs and stays hunched over his cigarette. The night's blown as far as he's concerned.

CHAPTER 20

Dr. Jo's show is pretty good tonight. As Albert, Stu, and I huddle together around the radio listening, we almost forget that there's a wild pool party going on just a hundred yards away.

Dr. Jo tries to be this real upbeat, cool kind of guy who's on a crusade to educate people about sex. Sometimes it's hard to believe the guy is for real, because he takes everything so seriously. Like a woman calls up and says the only time her husband will have sex with her is when *The Tonight Show* is on. This even gets a grin from bummed-out Albert. But Dr. Jo gets real serious and asks the woman why it bothers her and suggests that next time she try to change the channel on the TV and see what her husband does.

Then a guy calls up and says he's nineteen years old and still a virgin. He wants to know what he's missing. Boy, does that strike home for me. I listen carefully while Dr. Jo tells the guy that sex is a wonderful and satisfying experience, but that he shouldn't be upset if he hasn't had it yet. His time will come.

Stu winks at me.

People call up and talk about all kinds of crazy things. Is it okay to be bisexual?

"It's hard enough just to be sexual," Albert mutters.

A woman calls up and says her boyfriend likes to use whips

and chains. A gay guy calls up and complains that he doesn't like meeting other men in bathhouses.

"Bathhouses?" Albert scowls. The shower room here at the club is sometimes called the bathhouse.

"I don't think that's what he means," Stu says.

"What does he mean?" I ask.

"In the city there are places," Stu tells us. "They're like the old Roman baths. Gay guys hang around them and meet each other."

Albert and I nod. Sometimes I wonder how Stu knows stuff like that.

One surprising thing about the show is how many people our age or even younger call up with questions. I guess it's good because that way they can get the right answers to things instead of not knowing. A lot of times they'll say they're calling for a friend, but you get the feeling it's really their questions and they're just too embarrassed to admit it.

And then there are some really weird ones. Like girls who come home to find their boyfriends in bed with their mothers, and guys who find out that their fathers are gay. Actually, all that stuff makes for a pretty interesting show and the Dr. Jo Truth and Sex Radio Hour goes pretty fast. Before we know it, it's over and Gordy didn't get on.

"I read in a magazine that he gets something like three hundred calls every show and can only take about twenty of them," Albert says.

Stu nods. He looks disappointed.

It's around eleven o'clock now and kids are starting to leave the party, so we have to get their cars. Albert hangs around the valet shack and helps us. Considering that it's his night off, it's a pretty decent thing to do.

The pool party is supposed to end at twelve, but by the time everybody changes their clothes and gets their cars, it's closer to twelve thirty or even a quarter to one. Finally the parking lots are almost empty and the three of us and Bobby the part-timer are slumped on the bench, catching our breaths. It seems really quiet all of a sudden without the band and the noise of the party anymore. All we hear are the voices of the clean-up crew as they get the pool area ready for the daily invasion of mommies and kiddies tomorrow.

On the bench no one moves. I just keep thinking that it's too bad that Gordy didn't get to talk to Dr. Jo tonight. Now he's going to be weird again for another week.

Stu yawns.

"Got a date tonight?" Albert asks.

Stu grunts. "Yeah, with my bed."

The rest of us nod in agreement. Getting into bed sounds like the best thing in the world right now.

We're just about to get up when Gordy suddenly appears at the valet shack. He's wearing jeans and a blue polo shirt and he's got a towel over his shoulder. There's a short dark-haired girl with him. Kind of cute. A little on the chunky side. Big brown eyes.

Gordy looks real surprised. "Uh, what are you guys doing here?" he asks.

For a moment Stu, Albert, and I are totally confused.

"We're just finishing up work," I tell him.

"Yeah, and what are *you* doing here?" Albert asks.

Gordy gestures to the girl. "Well, uh, I just wanted to show Debbie here where I worked." Debbie smiles at us.

"But you were supposed to be calling Dr. Jo," Stu says.

"And how come you have a towel?" I ask.

"And how come your hair is wet?" Albert asks.

"Well, uh . . ." Gordy starts to stammer again.

Meanwhile Albert gets to his feet. Stu and I are right behind him.

"You were at the pool party, you turd."

Gordy starts to back away. "Well, I never said I wasn't going, guys. I just said I'd try to call Dr. Jo."

"But you didn't call him," Stu says angrily.

"That's because I met Debbie," Gordy explains in a trembling voice. (Debbie is scowling at him and us like she can't understand what we're talking about.) "You guys should be happy for me."

"We should be happy breaking our backs all night while you went to the pool party?" Stu asks. This could be the first time I've ever seen him truly furious.

"I was gonna try Dr. Jo from the party," Gordy whimpers.

Albert laughs. "Oh, you are a dead man."

Gordy turns and starts running, with the three of us right behind. We chase him across the parking lots and through the dark club grounds toward the beach. We chase him pretty far down the beach too, but the guy knows he's running for his life and he manages to keep his distance.

After a while we give up and turn back, gasping for breath.

"I didn't know he could run that fast," I wheeze.

"Or that far," Stu adds.

"Let's kill him tomorrow," Albert says as we walk back along the sand.

We get back to the parking lot and see that Gordy's friend Debbie is gone. So we search around and find Gordy's parents' Peugeot parked near the service entrance to the club. Gordy must have borrowed it for the night and parked it there because he figured we wouldn't see it. We let the air out of all the tires and head back to our own cars.

CHAPTER 21

I don't know what time it is when I finally get back to the parking lot. All I know is that it's late and I can't decide if I should really be angry at Gordy. I mean, tricking Stu into letting him have the night off was a completely conniving, stinking thing to do, but thinking about it now, it's kind of funny. There we were, worried all night that if Gordy didn't talk to Dr. Jo he was going to commit suicide because he played with himself too much. The guy really pulled a good one on us. And he still has to go home and explain to his parents why their car is up at the club with four flat tires.

It's dark and still in the lot. The loudest noise is the sound of gravel crunching under my sneakers and the distant grumble of engines starting as Stu and Albert get in their cars and head home. The door handle of the van feels cold as I pull it open and get in. The familiar smell of rotten leaves and grass clippings hits my nose as I put the key in the ignition and start her up.

"Oh, Scott!"

I jump so high that my head bangs against the ceiling of the van. Ow! Turning around, I see Paula, lying in the back.

"Jeez, you scared me," I tell her, rubbing the sore spot on my head.

Paula yawns and rubs her eyes. "I'm sorry. Didn't mean to. I guess I fell asleep." She gets up and comes in front and sits down next to me.

"Mind if I ask what you're doing here?"

"Christine took off with some guy. So I figured I could get a ride home with you."

I turn and shake my head wearily. "It's after one on a Sunday night. Don't you think your mother or Eddie might be wondering where you are?"

"My mother's probably out cold in front of the television and I told Eddie not to come over tonight," Paula says. "I'm sorry if I scared you, Scott. Really I am."

She reaches over and touches my arm lightly. Does she know what that does to me? It may be late and I may be tired, but I'm not *that* tired. Seventeen years of accumulated frustration starts to bubble up inside me. Just a foot away is Paula, my golden opportunity, my salvation, the answer to all my woes. If only I hadn't been born with a conscience.

"Want to go somewhere?" Paula asks innocently.

"Yeah, home," I tell her, switching on the van's lights and shifting into gear.

We pull out of the parking lot and Paula seems a little peeved. "Can I ask you something, Scott?"

"Yeah."

"Why do you always act like this? Like you're too good for me?" she says. "I know you like me. I can tell by the way you act and the way you look at me. Why do you fight it so much?"

I rub my eyes and try to think, but this is not exactly the best moment for a heart-to-heart conversation. I'm having a hard enough time just keeping my eyes open. As I pull onto the Post Road, in the dark distance I can see the Cordoba's taillights disappearing as Stu heads home.

"It's not that I think I'm too good for you, Paula," I tell her. "It's just that it's not gonna do either of us any good. You have a boyfriend and I have a girlfriend."

"I'm sick of Eddie," Paula says. "And it doesn't sound like you're so happy with, uh, what's-her-name."

"Alix." I remind myself that I have to pick her up at the

airport the day after tomorrow. "Actually, you're right. It doesn't have that much to do with them. It has to do with us, Paula. What makes you think I wouldn't just be interested in you for sex, like Eddie?"

Paula is quiet for a moment. "But I think you like me, and we haven't had sex."

"Yeah, well . . ." I'm beginning to see how this conversation could go around and around in circles without getting anywhere. The whole situation is crazy. Maybe I am being too serious. I mean, what's the big deal? Maybe we should just go make love and get it over with. Then tomorrow I could tell Paula it was all a mistake. I was just overcome with lust. She'll be a little hurt, but not too bad. She's been used for sex before. . . . Wait a minute.

"Paula, you know how you said you think Eddie only wants you for sex? Well, once guys know about your, uh, reputation, it's just gonna happen over and over again. I mean, there may be guys out there who'd honestly like you as a girlfriend, but even they can't be sure, because it all gets mixed up with their desire to have sex with you."

Paula doesn't answer right away. She lights a cigarette and thinks it over for a moment. Then she says, "Everyone makes it sound like sex is such a big deal. I don't even care that much about it. It's just nice to be close to someone and to be held sometimes, that's all. I swear, if I'd known everyone was going to make such a big deal out of it . . ." She shakes her head.

Too late now, I can't help thinking as I steer the van into our community. When I stop in front of Paula's house, she turns to me and I realize that there are tears in her eyes.

"What should I do, Scott?" she asks, sniffing.

She's asking me? I have no answer. She sniffs again and chokes a little on her tears. She's miserable and I feel awful. The only thing I can do is slide across the front seat and put my arm around her.

"Oh, Scott," she moans softly as she leans her head against my chest and sobs. "I hate to let anyone see me cry."

"It's okay," I whisper, hugging her gently. "I won't tell anyone."

CHAPTER 22

Gordy had to get a guy from a garage to help him with his parents' car the morning after the party. He said his parents were really mad at him. Not only that, but Stu says he has to work three weeks with no time off, as penance. That means the rest of us will have a couple of extra free nights.

The funny thing is, Gordy doesn't care one bit. He's in love. The night after the pool party Debbie spent the whole evening hanging around the valet shack with him. And during dinner break they went off down the beach somewhere. Gordy came back grinning like a fool.

Now Albert is the one who is super-depressed. He insists it has nothing to do with Gordy's good fortune, but the rest of us know better.

CHAPTER 23

Get this. I called the Shumans last night to tell them I'd pick up Alix at the airport today. So The Cold One tells me that I better come over this morning and get Alix's car. She can't stand the idea of her daughter riding anywhere in my van.

Actually, I don't mind. My van is so old that I'm always a little worrried that it's going to break down on the highway. And now that it's leaking oil, I guess I should be even more concerned.

So I go over to the Shumans' this morning (making sure to park on the street) and walk up the driveway. I pull the big brass knocker and let it bang against the front door and a couple of moments later The Cold One opens it. As usual she's dressed to kill. Even though it's only 9:30 A.M., she's wearing a striped caftan and she's all made up and she's got tons of jewelry on. Who does she get this dressed up for at nine thirty in the morning? The maid?

Stranger yet is the way she greets me. She actually has a smile on her face.

"Oh, Scott, come in," she says as sweet as honey.

I step in and she closes the door behind us. Now she leads me toward the kitchen, talking as we go.

"And how are your parents, Scott?"

"Uh, fine, Mrs. Shuman." Has she ever asked about my parents before? Does she even know I have parents?

"Oh, that's good," she says. In the kitchen she takes a set of keys out of a drawer and hands them to me. "It's so nice of you to pick up Alix."

"It's nothing," I tell her.

She opens the door to the carport. "Now, drive carefully. Don't speed."

"Uh, sure, Mrs. Shuman." The next thing I know, she closes the door behind me and I'm standing in the carport, totally confused. Who knows? Maybe she's taking some kind of pill that makes her nice or something. Well, I'm not going to complain. I get into the Benz, fire her up, and head out to the airport.

You should see the looks I get from the other drivers as I sail down the highway with the top down and my shades on. Guys look envious, girls smile, old dudes frown. The thing about a red Benz convertible is that you can't ignore it. Everyone has to react. I wonder how they'd react if they knew I was just playing chauffeur.

I leave the Benz in the airport parking lot and go into the terminal. Alix's plane is coming in from Boston at Gate 26 and I sit down in the waiting room with all the other boyfriends and girlfriends and parents and kids who are waiting for their loved ones. Does Alix still qualify as a loved one for me? Do I qualify for her? Did I receive a phone call or a letter or even a postcard from her during the two weeks she was away? The truth is, Alix isn't the letter-writing type. But still, I got no sense that she missed me. And did I miss her? Well, in a way. I missed being half of the Dynamic Duo, the solid, dedicated boyfriend and girlfriend, the handsome couple, the envy of everyone as we cruised down the Post Road in the Benz. I missed being identified as the guy who went with Alix Shuman. I missed looking out at the harbor at night from Alix's backyard. I missed that secure feeling of knowing that every girl around knew I was taken. I missed everything about going with Alix except one thing—I'm not sure I missed Alix herself.

They announce over the loudspeaker that Alix's flight from Boston has landed and is now disembarking. Around me people get up and press toward the airline gate. I get up and stand with them, as if it would be disrespectful to remain seated. As the loved ones start appearing they are greeted with hugs and kisses. It's kind of strange, considering they've only come in from Boston.

Finally I spot Alix coming down the corridor. There's that famous walk. She's as darkly tanned as I've ever seen her and the blond streaks in her hair have been bleached even blonder by the sun and seawater. She's wearing jeans and a blue Oxford shirt rolled up to the elbows, and as she walks, other girls' boyfriends turn their heads. Once again I feel proud that she's mine.

Only there's a problem. When Alix sees me, she gives me a look of ice. Shades of The Cold One!

"I don't want to talk to you," she says, walking right past me.

"Wait. What're you talking about? I came to pick you up."

"I'll take the airport limousine," Alix says.

"But I brought your car."

"Then you'll take the limousine."

We're walking down the corridor toward the baggage claim. Alix won't even look at me.

"Look, will you at least tell me what's wrong?" I ask.

"You already know, Scott."

"What do you mean I already know? If I knew, I wouldn't be asking, would I?"

"I heard all about you and that little slut," Alix says as we get onto an escalator.

Aha! So that's it. As incredible as it may seem, someone has already told her about Paula. But who? Who would be nasty and vindictive enough to call Alix all the way in Nantucket? Oh, no, I can't believe it. There's only one person. The Cold One. No wonder she was in such a good mood this morning.

"Look, I don't know what you've heard, but it's not true," I tell her. "Alix, you have to listen."

"You were just waiting for me to go away so that you could fool around with that girl," she says.

"That's not true, Alix. I don't know who you talked to or what they told you, but it's just not true."

We arrive at the baggage claim area and join the big crowd waiting for the luggage to come out. There are so many people pressed so close together that I stop talking. All of a sudden I can see everything slipping away—my beautiful girlfriend, the red Benz, the sailboat rides, the ski trips. For two years I've indentified myself with Alix and suddenly it's all disappearing.

In the crowd I move close to her.

"Look," I whisper. "Paula Finkel is my next-door neighbor and she's a messed up little kid and I was only spending some time with her to try to help her out."

"Since when did you become such a noble spirit?" Alix whispers back sarcastically.

"Alix, I wish you'd try to understand."

"Understand what? That the second I go away my boyfriend sneaks off with some fifteen-year-old tramp? You're really disgusting, Scott."

"I didn't sneak off anywhere with her," I say angrily. Unfortunately this comes out a little louder than I intended and a lot of people around us turn and stare.

Alix giggles, but I am mortified. It's one thing to have your girlfriend break up with you because you were fooling around with someone else. But it's crazy for your girlfriend to break up with you because you *weren't* fooling around.

A couple of bags that look like Alix's come around on the carousel and I reach over and grab them. Alix gives me an exasperated, angry look, but she doesn't try to tear them out of my hands. We start to walk toward the exit.

"I'm just going to take a wild guess," I tell her as I lug her bags out of the airline terminal and into the sunshine. "I bet you got a call from your mother and she told you all about me and Paula."

"I called Joanne Hawken and she confirmed it," Alix says.

"Confirmed what?" I ask. "That I took her fishing?"

"Joanne said she heard you two were out in some playground one night."

"It was the middle of the day and we were in the playground near our houses. Paula was upset and she needed to talk to me."

"About what, Scott?"

"You wouldn't believe it. Her mother's a drunk. She hits her. The kid is totally screwed up."

"And you thought you could help her?" Alix asks skeptically.

"Well, I figured I could listen. I mean, you weren't around and I didn't have anything better to do."

By the time we get out to Alix's car she's become a little more reasonable.

"You promise you won't see her anymore?" she asks as I open the trunk and put the bags in.

"Alix, we never *saw* each other that way to begin with."

"But now you won't see her at all, will you?"

In a moment of weakness, having just faced the possibility of being without a steady girlfriend for the first time in two years, I dumbly agree. Alix's victory smile is radiant. The breeze in the parking lot lifts her hair lightly. God, she's beautiful. For a moment I wonder how I ever could have thought of breaking up with her.

CHAPTER 24

"I'm calling my lawyer!" Mrs. Berman yells at me. She's standing in the driveway while I'm on my hands and knees on her front lawn with a trowel, a jam jar, and a can of beer. I've just buried half a dozen of these jars in the lawn and filled them with beer.

"But, Mrs. Berman, this is the best way to get rid of chinch bugs," I tell her. "They love the smell of beer and when they climb into the jar to taste it, they get drunk and fall in and drown."

"That's the most ridiculous thing I've ever heard," Mrs. Berman shouts in a high-pitched voice. "You're fired. Take those jars out of my lawn and leave. You'll be hearing from my lawyer." Then she turns and marches back into her house.

I get up and start digging up the jars. If that's what she wants, fine. Truth is, she hasn't been that happy with my lawn-care performance lately. No doubt the neighbors have been talking about the brown spots, the tree roots, etc. People probably stare when they pass on the sidewalk. And poor Mrs. Berman, who never did anything to anyone, has to take it all.

I really don't believe that she's going to sue me. I think she's just going to hire some big lawn-care company. With experts. By the end of the summer she'll spend more than she would on a new fur coat. And I guarantee you she'll still have the slimy spots and the roots. The chinch bugs may be gone, especially if the experts know about putting jars of beer in the lawn.

Okay, so that takes care of one lawn job this morning. Next stop, the Finkels'. But before I start on their lawn, I make a pit stop at my house to use the john and get a cold drink. Coming into the kitchen, I find Kerry sitting by the open window in her tennis clothes. She looks surprised to see me.

"Scott, what are you doing here?"

"Just came in to get something to drink," I tell her. It seems odd that she's inside today instead of out on the tennis courts. And why is she sitting so close to the open window?

"What are you doing, Kerry?"

My sister puts her finger to her lips. "Shh. Come and listen."

I sit down near the window. At first there's nothing, but then I hear someone yelling about pills. It's coming from the Finkel house—from Paula's window. It must be Mrs. Finkel. Then Paula yells back something about her mother having no right to look in her purse.

"What else have you got in here, you little whore?" Mrs. Finkel yells. Kerry and I look at each other.

Now we hear the sounds of drawers opening and slamming and Paula yelling that her mother has no right to go through her things. Then Paula's voice yelling, "Stop it! Stop it!"

Then, in an even higher pitch, "Ow! Stop it! You're hurting me!"

"What are you doing with those pills?" Mrs. Finkel screams.

"I . . . I was holding them for a friend."

"Liar! You're a lying little whore!"

"Oh, I hate you!" Paula screams. "I hate you so much!"

Kerry looks at me and rolls her eyes.

There's a loud slap as a door slams. Something crashes. I bet Mrs. Finkel slammed the door and Paula threw something at it. Now there's silence.

For a moment I just stare at the kitchen table. It's really shocking to hear stuff like that. It almost sounds like they're going to kill each other one of these days.

"Do you think Paula takes drugs?" Kerry asks in a low voice. I look up at her, puzzled. "What?"

"What her mother said about finding pills in her purse," Kerry says.

"I don't think it's those kind of pills," I tell her.

It takes Kerry a moment to figure it out. "Birth control pills?"

"That's my guess."

"Mrs. Finkel should be glad Paula takes them," Kerry says. "At least she won't have a baby."

"Not everyone thinks that way," I tell her.

Kerry looks back out the window. "Do you think Mrs. Finkel *really* hits Paula?" she asks.

"Yeah, I think she does," I tell her. "For all I know she uses a belt or something."

"God," Kerry says, making her eyes bulge out to signify disbelief. I know what she's thinking. No matter how bad we were as kids, our parents never hit us. Sent us to our rooms, yes. Grounded us for weeks, yes. But nothing like what's going on at the Finkels'. Up till now I would have sworn that kind of stuff only happened on television.

"I just wish we could do something," I mutter.

"Mom said we should stay out of it," Kerry says.

"So? Do you always have to agree with everything Mom says?"

"You said it was none of our business too."

She's got me there. I did, didn't I? But that was weeks ago, and now things have changed. I like Paula. I mean, it's not just that I feel sorry for her, or want to jump in the sack with her. Her problem is that she's honest and she doesn't play games. People can't deal with a fifteen-year-old girl who likes sex because it feels good to be close to someone. Is it Paula's fault that it's the only way she can get affection?

CHAPTER 25

The worst part is that I still have to go over there and cut their lawn. Right now I probably hate Mrs. Finkel as much as Paula does. I know that it can't all be her fault, but it's not a totally rational feeling.

I get the mower out of the van, start it up, and get to work. Every once in a while I glance at the front of the house to see if Mrs. Finkel or Paula is there, but no one comes to the window. So I mow onward, inhaling the fumes and crisp smell of freshly cut grass. Sometimes when I cut grass I feel like a machine pushing another machine. A robot could be programmed to push a mower back and forth across a lawn. I wish I was a robot now so I wouldn't have to think about Paula.

After I finish the front, I start on the side of the house where Paula's room is. She must hear the mower engine and realize I'm out here working. Sure enough, she sticks her head out of the window as I pass. She's got a swollen bruise on her left cheekbone, and her eyes are reddened. God, it makes me mad to see that.

"Hi, Scott."

I stop pushing the mower and turn the throttle down.

"How're you doing?" I ask.

"Not so good."

"What happened to your face?"

"I bumped it," Paula lies. She doesn't know that Kerry and I listened to the fight.

"How come you're not out by the pool?" I ask, glancing up at the sun and blue sky. "It's pretty nice out today."

"My mother says I have to stay in my room."

"How long?"

"Probably until I run away."

"When are you gonna do that?" I ask.

"Not till this bump on my face goes down a little."

"Where're you gonna go?"

Paula rests her elbows on the windowsill and shrugs. "I don't know. North Carolina, maybe."

I know I shouldn't say what comes out of my mouth next, but I can't help it. "I don't know why you didn't go down there a long time ago."

Paula looks surprised. But then she says, "I guess because Eddie's here. And besides, I don't know if my father would really want me. He has a new wife and kids and everything. He probably has enough on his hands."

"Does he know the way your mother treats you?"

Paula shakes her head. "I tried to tell him. But I don't think he really believed me. Besides, it's never been like this before. I don't know what's bothering her lately, but she's really gotten crazy."

"You have to get out of there," I tell her.

Suddenly Paula looks scared. "But what about Eddie?"

"What about him?" I ask. "You said all he wants you for is sex, right?"

Paula looks away and doesn't answer. I swear I don't get it. One day she tells me she doesn't want him anymore and the next day she can't leave him. Now fresh tears come to her eyes. I look down at the ground. Maybe I've been too hard on her. Maybe it's not what Eddie wants her for that's important; maybe it's what she needs him for. That's how bad it is—the only person in the world she feels close to is someone who just uses her for sex.

I glance back at my house to make sure no one's in the kitchen watching us. Then I look back at Paula, who's wiping her eyes. What can I offer her that's any better? Words of encouragement? Somehow I get the feeling that's not what she needs late at night when her mother is passed out in front of the tube. One thing my mother always told me to do when I couldn't understand something was to put myself in the other person's shoes and see how I'd react. Suppose I was a fifteen-year-old girl with no available father and a drunken mother who sometimes hit me? I think I'd be scared out of my gourd too.

"Listen," I tell her. "If you ever decide you want to go see your father, let me know. I'll help you get down there."

Paula just nods. Somehow I get the feeling it doesn't mean anything to her.

CHAPTER 26

There's been a change in the Tauscher family's attitude toward Eddie's morning escape routine. For a while it was the big breakfast event. At 8:15 every eye was aimed at Paula's window. It seemed like breakfast wasn't complete unless we got to see Eddie. And on the mornings when he didn't appear, there was always this funny feeling. Was something wrong? Did they have a fight? It was like a soap opera.

But lately it's changed. We've started to pretend that we're no longer interested. We act like nothing is going on, like only a bunch of nosy perverts would sit at breakfast every morning waiting for some greasy guy to crawl out of a fifteen-year-old girl's window. We wouldn't be interested in *that*. Not the Tauschers.

But of course we all still are. None of us can really resist peeking over there.

As breakfast begins this morning my mother is real excited. There's a women's satellite tournament in White Plains and for the first time ever she's going to be the umpire instead of just a lineswoman. That means she gets to sit in the high chair and call out the scores and boss the players around. And because the tournament is part of the satellite tour (halfway between the

local country club championship and Wimbledon) it may get
some space in *The New York Times* or one of the tennis magazines. My mother's name may even get mentioned.

I hate to take the wind out of her sails, but . . .

"Uh, listen," I tell everyone around the table. "I know I once
said that what goes on next door is none of our business, but I
think maybe I've changed my mind."

My father looks up from his eggs and asks, "Why, Scott?"

"Well, mostly because I found out that not only does Mrs.
Finkel hit the bottle, but she really hits Paula too. Kerry and I
heard them fighting yesterday and later I saw Paula. Her cheek
was swollen and she had scratches on her face."

"Do you know what they were fighting about?" my mother
asks.

"Birth control pills," Kerry tells her.

My mother and father cast questioning glances at each other.
Then my father looks at me. "What do you think we should do,
Scott?"

"Well, her father lives in North Carolina. I thought maybe we
could get in touch with him. And I always hear this ad on the
radio about child abuse. It's some kind of social service you can
call."

My parents listen, but neither is in a rush to run to the phone.

"I'm telling you, her mother really hits her," I tell them.
"Kerry and I both heard it and I saw her face."

"Did *she* tell you that her mother hit her?" my father asks.

"No, she's afraid to say it, but it's so obvious. I mean, we
heard her yelling that her mother was hurting her." Next to me
Kerry nods in agreement.

My father thinks it over for a moment and then puts down his
fork. "Scott, different people have different ways of dealing with
their problems. When I was growing up, my father used to spank
me. Sometimes he even used a paddle. Of course, that's not the
way we've brought up you and Kerry, but everybody has his own
way of doing things. Now, I know you mean well and are concerned about Paula, but it is difficult to interfere in such a per-
sonal situation. We all see what goes on over there in the morn-

ing and we know that Paula is a difficult child. It may be that
this is the way Mrs. Finkel chooses to deal with her."

"But Mrs. Finkel is drunk all the time," I tell him.

"We hardly know that to be a fact," my mother says.

"So you're just going to sit back and wait until something
really bad happens?" I ask in disbelief.

"Scott," my mother says, "sometimes you just can't interfere
with other people's lives."

Suddenly I feel really mad. "You don't believe Mrs. Finkel hits
Paula."

"Yes, we do," my mother says.

"But you don't believe that she *really* hits her. You just think
it's some kind of punishment or something."

"How can you be so certain that it's not?"

How can I? Jeez, what a bunch of narrow-minded, self-cen-
tered jerks. I push my chair back.

"Where are you going?" my mother asks.

"Upstairs." I turn and go up the stairs two steps at a time and
slam my bedroom door. A week from now Paula Finkel may be
dead because my parents think what's going on over there is
none of their business. I kick off my sneakers and flop down on
my bed and stare up at the ceiling. There's a picture of Bill
Murray grinning down at me. It seems like I must have put it up
there a hundred years ago, but I've never bothered to take it
down. I think I put it up originally because he was a pretty funny
guy, but now I leave it up to remind me that when things seem
to be really serious, it helps to remember there's a funny side to
everything too. Except at the moment I can't think of anything
funny about my parents and what's going on next door. Maybe
this is the exception to the rule.

I don't know how long I've been lying there, staring up at Bill
Murray, when I hear footsteps coming up the stairs. Then
there's a knock on my door. It must be my mother or Kerry.

"Yeah, come in," I yell.

The door opens and my father comes in. My eyes immediately
jump to the clock next to my bed. It's almost nine. That's weird,
he's usually on his way to the office by now.

My father pulls the chair from my desk, turns it around, and straddles it backward, the way detectives on TV do. He even looks like a detective in his tie and vest, with his shirt sleeves rolled up. I wonder if he's going to handcuff me and shine a light in my eyes.

"Scott, I don't want to give you the wrong impression," he says. "Both your mother and I are concerned about what goes on next door. It's just . . ." He seems to be having trouble finding the words.

"Just what, Dad?"

"Well, it's just that we don't understand your, er, sudden interest in the Finkel girl."

"I think we should do something before she really gets hurt, that's all."

My father blinks. "Have you, uh, been spending much time with her, Scott?"

What? How does he know I've been spending any time at all with her? Oh, yeah, Kerry. Miss Mouth.

"Not much, but some. I mean, I took her fishing one day and I run into her sometimes."

"That's all?" my father asks skeptically.

All of a sudden I'm getting funny vibes from him. "What's your point?" I ask.

"Well . . ." My father pauses and clears his throat. "You've got to be careful when you, uh, fool around with a girl like her, Scott. I mean, I was once a teenager and I know what it's like. And I imagine that a girl like Paula can be quite a temptation. But you must keep in mind that just one mistake can have a devastating effect on your life."

All I can do is stare at him. I don't know whether to laugh or what. "You think the only reason I've shown any concern about Paula Finkel is because I'm trying to get into her shorts?"

My father looks uncomfortable. "Well, it just seems like a possible explanation. The girl has lived next door for two years and you've never shown any interest before. And I'm not blaming you, son. I know what being a teenager is like. All I'm saying is, please be careful."

God, I wish he'd stop telling me he knows what being a teenager is like, because if he really knew, he would understand this a hell of a lot better. This is the kind of crap I expect to get from Albert, not from my own father.

"Listen, Dad," I tell him. "I really don't think you have to worry about any illegitimate grandchildren running around here, okay?"

My father looks relieved.

"But it would be nice if you could give me a little more credit sometimes," I add.

"Of course I give you credit, Scott," he says. He starts to get up. Mission accomplished; it's time to sell plastic ornaments.

"Hey, Dad," I say just as he reaches the door. "Do you make any plastic brides that look like pregnant teenagers?"

My father's jaw drops, but then I wink at him. "Only kidding, Pop."

CHAPTER 27

A couple of days later, on my day off, Alix and I are stretched out on a blanket at the beach. Alix is listening to music on her radio, as are most of the other kids lying on the blankets and towels around us. Fortunately by some unspoken agreement among the radio operators, all are on the same channel or else there'd be mass confusion.

As the smell of marijuana smoke wafts through the air, concentrated tan maintenance is the order of the day. I look at the bodies around us and I can't help thinking of one of those *National Geographic* specials where you see all these seals lying on the rocks, sunning themselves. I feel somewhat uncomfortable, lying here several shades whiter than most of the seals around me, but working full-time is not conducive to tan development.

Something else is making me even more uncomfortable. It's been a week since Alix returned from Nantucket, but it doesn't feel like she and I have gotten back together. It almost seems like there's an invisible shield between us, keeping us apart. We might as well be strangers. And it's not that I'm angry or mad at her. I just don't feel *anything* toward her. We're doing the same things we did before, but there's nothing there.

Next to me Alix stirs as a new song comes on the radio. She's been complaining all summer how much she hates this particular song, so it doesn't surprise me that she reaches over and turns the volume down. I don't know what she plans to do about the other sixty radios around us still playing the song full blast. But having turned the volume down, she doesn't resume roasting position. Instead she leans on her elbow, turned toward me.

"Who was with you in the van that night after the pool party?"

I take a deep breath and let out a sigh. "I thought the KGB only followed people in Russia."

"Scott, I just want to know one thing," Alix says. "Did you?"

"Did I what?"

"Don't play games. You know."

God, this is so unbelievable. My father, my sister, my girlfriend, my other friends. They all think the same way.

"Scott?"

I turn and squint at her. "No, I didn't. But I swear, if I'd known how much trouble everyone was going to give me, I probably would have."

"That's disgusting." Alix turns away from me. I close my eyes and watch the pictures the sun makes behind my eyelids. Do I really need this?

Later I go into the water. Maybe I'll get into good enough shape so that the next time Paula and I race, I'll beat her. Ha, ha, that's supposed to be a joke. But as I swim I think it's interesting that once again Paula's on my mind. I really don't think she has that much to do with what is happening between Alix and me. No, what's happened to us is that we've just about hit the end of puppy love. At least I have.

There's a rope that marks the boundary of the swimming area and I sort of hang on it and float on my back, looking up at the sky. What if Alix and I did break up? What if I was no longer half of the Dynamic Duo? I'd still be Scott Tauscher, for better or for worse. Things really wouldn't be that different. I mean, it's been so long since we enjoyed anything together. Would it really kill me if I never got to ride in the Benz or went skiing at her parents' chalet again?

I float out there for a while and then swim back in. The water feels good, but I'm starting to feel soggy. For a moment, back at the beach, I can't find Alix or our blanket. Then I realize what's happened.

She's gone.

CHAPTER 28

Tonight Stu and I go to the miniature golf course at Playland. I've made no effort to talk to Alix since she left me at the beach. I'm not even mad. I'm sad. Sad because it's finally over. The first big romance of my life. The worst part of the whole thing is knowing that in a week, or two weeks, or a month, I'm going to see the Benz somewhere and a new guy is going to be sitting in the passenger seat.

There is no doubt in my mind that Stu is the person I want to be with tonight. Albert wouldn't be sympathetic. He'd probably say something like I'd never slept with Alix so it couldn't matter that much. Gordy would be just the opposite. He'd probably suggest that we jump off a bridge together. Even though I'm not as close to Stu as I am to those guys, I still feel like he'll understand better.

It's Stu's idea to play miniature golf. I guess he knows that it's better than sitting around in some bar getting smashed. Besides, I'm not sure there is a hell of a lot to say anyway.

Playland is this big carnival sort of place with games and rides and, of course, miniature golf. It turns out that Stu is amazing with a putter in his hands. We play a couple of rounds and there is no hole that he can't complete in just two shots. I lose count of how many holes-in-one he gets. I'm so concerned with trying

to keep up with him that I even forget about Alix. The only good
thing about playing with Stu is that he doesn't make you feel bad
about not being as good as he is. He just lets me take my time.

We finish two rounds, get a couple of beers, and sit down at a
small redwood picnic table near the booth where people pick up
their balls and putters. It's a warm, sticky kind of night and I'm
reminded of something.

"You know, this is where Alix and I went on our first date the
summer after ninth grade," I tell him. "It seems so long ago. You
know what I'll never forget?"

"What?"

"It took me the whole summer just to get her to open her
mouth when I kissed her."

Stu's eyebrows rise slightly.

"And then when I'd try to French kiss her, I'd stick my
tongue in her mouth and I couldn't find her tongue anywhere. It
was like it had disappeared."

Stu chuckles and I shake my head. But inside I feel stupid. It's
like I've just done a little comedy routine, a little rap about the
prude who wouldn't French kiss. It sounds like something Albert
would say. It really has nothing to do with Alix and me, or the
fact that I really liked her and maybe, for a while, even loved her.

Somehow I think Stu must sense this because he asks, "How
come you broke up, Scott?"

I take a deep breath. "I guess we got to the point where we
were just replaying the same bad scenes over and over again.
Until she went away to Nantucket I never realized how mechanical I was, always feeling like I had to act a certain way and do
certain things. Have you ever felt that way?"

Stu thinks about it. He never answers a question without
thinking it over first. But before he can answer, something else
catches our attention. There's a guy and a woman making noise
out on the twelfth hole. He's dressed kind of like a golfer with a
yellow sport shirt and bright green pants. She's wearing a white
blouse and jeans and she looks bored and upset and embarrassed
because he's making a big deal about knocking a dumb little ball
into a hole in the ground.

Stu and I can hear him all the way across the course. "Come on, Betsy, hold the club the way I showed you. . . . No, that's not it. . . . Oh, my God, look at the way you're standing. . . . Of course it didn't go in the hole. This is golf, not hockey!"

Stu and I watch them progress from hole to hole. At the fourteenth the guy starts yelling even louder. Betsy looks pretty upset. It's hard to believe that anyone could take miniature golf so seriously.

At the sixteenth hole a little argument erupts between them. Betsy complains that she's getting tired of him trying to show her the right way and asks why they can't just have fun. Now her boyfriend gets real defensive and says he's only trying to help make her a better miniature-golf player.

"Unbelievable," Stu mutters, crumpling his empty beer cup and sinking it into a trash can about fifteen feet away.

"What a jackass, huh?"

Stu nods. "Listen, Scott. I want to try something. Just play along, okay?"

"Try what?"

"You'll see," he says, taking out his wallet.

By the time the guy and Betsy finish the eighteenth hole, they look like they're about to kill each other. As they come toward the putter rack to put their clubs away, Stu suddenly says to me in a loud voice, "You sure you don't want to play for ten bucks? It'll make the game more fun."

I don't have a clue to what he's talking about, but he's making a face at me like he wants me to say no.

"Uh, no, Stu, I don't want to."

Stu gives me a big wink.

"Oh, come on," he says. "It's just ten bucks." Again he makes a face at me.

"Uh, I don't want to," I tell him. What's he doing?

Another wink. Meanwhile out of the corner of my eye I see that the guy with Betsy is listening.

"Why not?" Stu asks loudly. "Neither of us is any good. It'll make the game more interesting."

"No," I tell him.

Suddenly the guy with Betsy turns to Stu and says, "I'll play you."

Stu acts surprised, like he hadn't noticed the guy before. He looks at his green pants and yellow shirt and acts like he doesn't know what to say.

Betsy is trying to pull her boyfriend away. "Come on, Frank, you've had enough golf tonight."

But Frank shakes her off. "Look," he tells her, "I'll play one round. It won't take long and you can get some cotton candy." He turns back to Stu. "Want to play for twenty?"

"That's too much," Stu says nervously. "How about fifteen?"

"It's a deal," Frank says. He reaches into his pocket and gives a couple of dollars to Betsy, who shrugs and goes off in search of cotton candy.

Frank and Stu get ready to tee off and I have to restrain myself from laughing out loud when Stu acts real dumb and nervous. This guy Frank is eating it up. He has a big grin on his face like he thinks this is going to be the easiest fifteen bucks he ever made.

They start to play the course. Frank is okay, but he's not nearly as good as Stu can be. I say "can be" because all of a sudden Stu can hardly get a par and he double bogies most of the holes. It must be nerves or something.

They've almost finished the course when Betsy returns with her cotton candy and a Coke. She sits down next to me at the picnic table and I can smell a heavy dose of perfume. She must be in her early twenties and her white blouse is open pretty far down. I can't help sneaking a peek.

"Who's winning?" she asks, catching me looking down her blouse.

I immediately straighten up and feel my face turn red. "Frank's killing him."

Betsy sighs. "I wish he'd lose. It would teach him a lesson."

Real great relationship these two have.

Frank and Stu finish the course and Frank is grinning from ear to ear as they walk back to the picnic table.

"Forty-one to fifty-three," he announces loudly as he waits for

Stu to peel fifteen dollars out of his wallet. I just stare at Stu. I can't believe he lost to that nerd.

Meanwhile Stu is shaking his head. "I just had some real bad luck. I'm usually much better than that. I don't know what happened."

Frank looks at him. "Tell you what. How about another round? Double or nothing?"

"Well, uh, what about your friend?" Stu asks, nodding toward Betsy.

Frank grins at her. "Aw, she don't mind as long as she got her cotton candy. Right, baby?"

Betsy shakes her head. I get the feeling she doesn't really want to be with him right now.

"Well, okay," Stu says.

They go back and start another round. I still don't understand what's going on. This time Stu plays a little better, but not nearly as well as he can play. He makes one or two really good shots, but Frank still keeps a comfortable lead. Everytime Stu sinks a good shot, I can almost read the word "luck" on Frank's lips.

Meanwhile, at the picnic table, Betsy eats her cotton candy and sips her Coke. Around the thirteenth hole she turns and asks me what the score is.

"Frank's up by five," I tell her.

"If your friend is so bad, why does he play for money?" she asks.

All I can do is shrug. "You got me."

Frank and Stu finish the second game about the same time Betsy finishes her cotton candy. I can see that she's eager to leave now. Frank comes off the course triumphant again. Stu follows, still muttering to himself.

"Thirty bucks!" Frank says. He even hugs Betsy.

"Okay, Frank, let's go," she says.

But Stu keeps muttering. "I just don't know what's wrong. I really am a better player than that, aren't I, Scott?"

"Yeah, you are," I say. But not tonight.

Betsy has grabbed Frank's arm and she's trying to pull him away, but Frank stops.

"Tell you what," he says, the little cogs in his brain whirring. "I'll forget the thirty bucks you owe me. Let's play one more round. For a hundred."

"Oh, come on, Frank." Betsy tugs at him. "You've played enough already."

But Frank doesn't budge. "What do you say?"

"Well, uh . . ." Stu seems uncertain. "A hundred is pretty steep. How about five dollars a point? Winner takes the difference."

Frank shakes his head. "Either we play for a hundred or I take my thirty now."

Stu still looks uncertain. How could he even think about playing the guy for a hundred when he's playing this badly? But now he takes out his wallet to count what he has. I look over his shoulder and see a lot of green in there. Frank sees it too.

So does Betsy, and her grip on Frank's arm seems to loosen.

"Okay," Stu says. "But I'm warning you, I'm better than these last two games. I swear it."

Frank grins. "Sure, sure," he says.

This game starts off like the others. Frank takes the lead early. But unlike before, Stu doggedly keeps up with him. He may fall one or two strokes behind, but never more than that, and as they get to the ninth hole Frank begins to look worried. True, he is ahead, but Stu is close enough to overtake him at any time.

On the eleventh hole Frank misses two easy putts and suddenly he and Stu are tied. For the next few holes they play almost even. Frank nervously makes a couple of easy mistakes, but Stu seems nervous too. By the fifteenth hole they are still even.

At the picnic table Betsy, who couldn't have cared less before, is now a regular cheerleader yelling, "Go, Frank, go!"

On the sixteenth hole Frank misses another easy putt. Stu makes his and goes ahead by one stroke. Frank starts cursing now, blaming himself for his easy mistakes. I notice Betsy's mood abruptly changes.

Frank misses another easy putt on the seventeenth and Stu goes ahead by two strokes. But then he misses an easy shot and falls back to a one-stroke lead. I have to admit that I'm as nervous as everyone else by now. After all, a hundred dollars is a hefty hunk of change.

But Frank's game falls apart on the eighteenth hole, where he misses three shots in a row. He finally gets so mad that he hits the ball as hard as he can, driving it right off the course, across the boardwalk, and out onto the beach. He comes back to the picnic table cursing himself and complaining that he never played so badly in his life. I watch as he forks over the hundred to Stu. The guy is truly pissed. It never occurs to him that Stu might be the better player. He thinks Stu just got lucky.

Betsy isn't too pleased either. "Well, well, the great miniature-golf player," she says sarcastically.

"Aw, shut up before I slam ya," Frank threatens her.

The two of them go off fuming at each other while Stu counts the money to make sure it's all there. Then he slides his putter back into the rack and sits down next to me.

"I don't get it," I tell him.

"Don't get what?"

"Why you just did that. I mean, if he hadn't blown his cool, you would have been out a hundred bucks."

Stu smiles. "You think so?"

Wait a minute. Is he implying that he played badly those first two games just to hustle Frank? I feel my jaw drop. Stu pulled it off so smoothly he even had me fooled. But . . .

"I needed the money," Stu says, as if he can read my mind.

"Why?" I ask. "I saw your wallet. It was full."

Stu takes out his wallet. "What, this?" he asks, opening it and taking out seven one-dollar bills folded in half so that both edges show.

All I can do is stare at him with my mouth open. I can't believe this. Stu hustling miniature golf?

"Hey, Scott, come on," he says, patting me on the shoulder. "What's the difference between that and taking ten bucks off some drunk for driving him five minutes home from the club?"

"There's a difference."

His smile disappears. He looks at me for a second and then starts to walk toward the exit.

Damn! I didn't mean to hurt his feelings. "Hey, Stu, wait!" I catch up to him. "Look, I didn't mean to hassle you, but I just don't get it."

Stu shrugs. "There's nothing to get, Scott. I told you I needed the money. Frank wanted to play and I obliged him. Anyway, don't have a heart attack about it. I don't do it very often."

"Why not?"

"Because it would be too easy to get my teeth smashed, that's why," Stu says as we walk through the Playland gates. "All you have to do is pick the wrong guy once, or the same guy twice. Next year I won't remember Frank, but you can bet he'll remember me."

We reach the parking lot. To tell you the truth, I'm kind of glad to get out of there before Frank figures out he's been hustled.

"So where are we going now?" I ask as we get into the Cordoba.

Stu gazes steadily at me. "I thought I might corrupt you some more. But not if you're going to give me a hard time about it."

"Who, me?" I answer with a grin.

CHAPTER 29

Corrupt me? I don't know what he's talking about, but I guess I'll see soon enough. Riding in the Cordoba, I've got to admit it still bothers me that Stu pulled that stunt, even on a jerk like Frank. But there are other things on my mind too. Like, if I wasn't with Stu, I'd be sitting in my room wondering if I was doing the right thing by not calling Alix, and worrying about what life was going to be like without her. I might even start missing her.

Stu is driving toward the harbor. I glance into the backseat and notice that someone has recently glued a pair of sunglasses onto the panda. Who would have thought Stu was such a character? Hustling miniature golf and driving around with that thing in his backseat.

Down in the harbor we pull into a dark marina that I've never been in before. It's after ten now and the evening is quieting down as night slips in. Stu gets out of the car and I follow him down onto the dock. There are a lot of houseboats in this marina. The slips are set up with electricity and running water.

Stu stops next to one houseboat. There are lights on inside, but the windows are covered with curtains. I hear music. Stu reaches into his pocket and takes out the hundred dollars he won from Frank. In the dark he tries to hand some of it to me.

"What's this?" I ask.

"Your cut," he says.

"You won it," I tell him, refusing to take it.

Stu shrugs and heads down onto the boat. Inside five guys are sitting around a table playing cards. I recognize a couple of them as graduates of my school. A couple of others look older and I don't recognize them. They turn around as we come in.

"Yo, Stu."

"Hey, you're early tonight."

"Pull up a chair, sport."

As we get closer, Stu introduces me. "Guys, this is Scott Tauscher."

When he says that, one guy whose back is to me turns around. Surprise, surprise. It's Shawn Shuman, Alix's brother.

There's a cigarette hanging out of the corner of his mouth, the smoke curling up into his eyes, making him squint. "Hey, Scott."

"Hi, Shawn."

Shawn turns back to the rest of the guys at the table. "This is the kid who goes with my sister," he tells them. "What's it been, Scott, two years?"

I nod dumbly. Somehow I have the feeling this isn't the time to tell him that Alix and I have just broken up. Meanwhile the other guys around the table look at me. If they don't know Alix personally, they've at least heard of her. I can almost read their minds: Any guy who's gone with Shawn's sister for two years is probably okay.

"Why don't you guys go into the kitchen and grab a couple of chairs," Shawn tells us.

I follow Stu into the kitchen. It's a mess. Empty beer and liquor bottles lying all over the counters, dirty dishes and empty ice trays in the sink, half-full bags of potato chips and pretzels, ashtrays overflowing with butts. I get the feeling it's been one continuous party on this boat for the last month and a half.

"Stu," I whisper as he opens the refrigerator, "I don't play poker."

Stu looks at me. "You know what a pair is?"

I nod.

"A straight?" Stu asks.

"Yeah."

"A flush?"

"Something the toilet does."

Stu smirks. "Why don't you watch for a while? You're welcome to play, or I'll take you home." He pulls a couple of beers out.

"Stu, how many nights a week do you play here?" I ask.

He scratches his head. "Oh, maybe five or six. Why?"

"Just wondering."

Back in the living room we sit down at the table and Stu exchanges his money for chips. It's a serious poker table, covered with green felt and with gullies for the chips. It is also a serious poker game. Nobody is making conversation. They just smoke and drink and play cards. It's so smoky in here that my eyes begin to water.

Stu gets dealt in. With each hand he shows me his cards, but it's hard for me to keep my mind on the game. Not only am I half suffocating from the smoke, but I keep thinking that this is how Stu's been spending all those nights we thought he was out chasing girls. Chasing chips instead.

As the game continues I see through the smoke that Stu is doing pretty well. He probably won't have to borrow any money from me this week. Shawn, on the other hand, seems to lose almost every hand. This is how the Shuman golden boy spends his old man's cash.

Around eleven I hear footsteps outside and three girls come in carrying grocery bags. Two are blondes whom I don't recognize. They look like sisters. The third is a dark-haired girl named Janet who just graduated from my school. Every guy in the school knows her. I'm sure that if a poll was taken on the sexiest girls around, she'd be one of the top five.

"How're you guys doing?" Janet asks loudly. One of her trademarks is her loud voice and inclination to say outrageous things.

"Okay, Jan."

"Yeah, fine." They don't even look up from the game.

Janet chuckles. "This is Lauren and Eileen," she says, gesturing to the two girls with her. "They're both from Ohio and they're staying with their aunt for the summer."

The guys at the table nod and mutter a few hellos, but they hardly glance up from their cards. I do look and notice that both girls have cute turned-up noses and corn-silk hair. Midwestern beauty-contest types. They follow Janet into the kitchen.

Stu nudges me back into the game. "You want in?"

I shake my head.

"Want me to take you home?" he asks.

"No, I don't mind watching," I tell him. Mostly because I'm not in a rush to get home.

Another half hour passes, and not only do I feel like I've inhaled two packs' worth of someone else's cigarette smoke, but I'm hungry too. So I get up and go into the kitchen.

The three girls are sitting at the kitchen table, which has been cleared off. In fact, the whole kitchen looks considerably cleaner. Janet is smoking a cigarette and talking about going to college, while the two corn-silk beauties listen. Neither is smoking. They're all wearing jeans and canvas shoes or sneakers. The Ohio girls are wearing light cotton sweaters. Janet is wearing a low-cut designer sweatshirt.

"Is there anything around to eat?" I ask, feeling the gaze of all three girls as I walk in.

"Plenty," Janet says, "if you happen to like soggy potato chips."

"As a last resort," I reply, and open the refrigerator. In short order I discover all the necessary ingredients for a cheese sandwich on slightly stale rye bread. I go to work on the kitchen counter, aware that the girls are watching me.

"Don't you go out with Shawn's sister, Alix?" Janet asks.

"Uh, yeah." Again, it doesn't seem like the appropriate time to announce to the world that Alix and I have split up.

"What's your name?"

"Scott Tauscher."

"Scott, did anyone ever tell you that you have wonderful eyebrows?"

The Ohio girls giggle.

Janet continues her interrogation. "So whose friend are you?"

"Stu Chock's."

Janet turns to the girls and rolls her eyes. "The good-looking blond. Tall, silent type."

Twittering from the Ohio girl section. Janet is actually a loud, pushy tease, and these nice Ohio girls are the perfect audience for her. She takes a puff on her cigarette and blows smoke up into the air, playing Ms. Sophisticated Know-It-All.

"So, Scott," she says, "who do you think should carry the burden of responsibility for birth control in a relationship?"

This is a typical Janet question—designed to embarrass me, entertain her friends, and make her out to be a big shot.

"The parents," I reply, taking a cold beer and my cheese sandwich out onto the deck for fresh air.

Except for an occasional thunderstorm it seems like this whole summer has been an almost continuous series of hot, bright days and warm, clear nights. Tonight the moon is just a sliver and the dark sky is awash with stars. The air and water are almost still. I push a couple of deck chairs around and then sit down in one and put my feet up on the other. I've got my beer in one hand and my sandwich in the other and I've just lost my first true girl friend. Things could be better, but they could be worse too.

I sit back and take a bite out of the sandwich and realize that I've positioned my chair so that it faces across the harbor. Up on the hill are brightly lit houses, and one of them, although I can't be exactly sure which, is Alix's.

"Nice night," someone says behind me. I turn and see that it's one of the girls from Ohio.

"Uh, yeah, it is," I reply. "I'm sorry, I forgot your name."

"Lauren," she says, standing on the deck and gazing at the dark water. "You know, this is the first time I've ever been to the ocean."

"Well, it's not really the ocean here."

"I know, but it's connected to the ocean."

"Where'd you meet Janet?" I ask.

"At my aunt's club. Isn't she a stitch?"

"I guess you could call her that. Hey, listen, want to sit down?" I offer her the chair I had my feet on.

"Thanks," Lauren sits down properly, not slouched, one leg crossed over the other, her hands in her lap.

"So, uh, how'd you manage to escape?" I ask.

Lauren smiles. "Janet and my sister decided to smoke a joint. Too much smoke."

"You don't indulge?" I ask.

"It makes me sleepy."

"How do you like it here?"

"I love the water," she says. "My aunt has a house right on the beach. At night you go to sleep listening to the waves."

"It sounds nice," I tell her. And she sounds nice too. Natural and relaxed. No big act, no BS. "What do you think of easterners?"

"Some are okay, some aren't," she replies. "The ones I can't stand are the ones who treat me like I'm a little country hick because I come from Ohio."

"Anyone in particular?"

"Guess."

I smile. "That's just the way she is."

"She treats us like we're such babes in the woods," Lauren says. "Eileen, my sister, loves it. But I swear I feel like telling Janet a few things that would open her eyes."

"Like what?"

Lauren winks at me. "If there's one difference between easterners and midwesterners, it's that you talk about things more. Things that don't seem like anyone's business to us."

I agree, but I still can't help wondering what sort of things she means.

For a while we just sit, looking at the starlit ripples in the water. It must be getting late now, but I'm still in no rush to go home.

"Janet said your girlfriend is stunning," Lauren says.

"Well, just between you and me," I tell her, "as of about two o'clock this afternoon she ceased being my girlfriend."

"Did you have a fight?"

"No, not really. It's probably been over for a long time, but it wasn't until this afternoon that we realized it."

Lauren looks closely at me. "Are you unhappy?"

"Yes and no. I mean, I'm glad it's over but it's sad to see it end."

"I know what you mean," she says. "I wasn't going to come east with Eileen this summer because of my boyfriend, but the same thing happened. It just ended one day. Now I'm glad I went away."

"You don't miss him?"

"Sometimes I do. But I try to keep busy and not think about it. It helps if you just keep doing things."

I nod. "Thanks for the tip."

Out over the water the sea gulls circle and squawk in the dark. There's a brief streak of light in the sky—a shooting star. Lauren and I both see it and quietly watch for another. I feel like we have something in common.

Later, much later, Stu comes out on the deck. Lauren and I have been sitting there for a long time. My neck hurts from looking up at the sky for so long.

"Come on, cowboy," he says, yawning and glancing at Lauren. "Let's get some rest."

I get up. My legs are stiff from sitting so long. Lauren yawns.

"I gotta get home and get some sleep," I tell her. "You need a ride?"

Lauren shakes her head. "I better go see what my sister is up to."

I know Stu is waiting, but I feel like I don't want to leave her. "Uh, listen, do you have a phone number or something?"

"My aunt's name is Wax," Lauren says. "It's the only one in the phone book."

Stu drives slowly, leaning up against the steering wheel. I'd be nervous if there was a lot of traffic, but there's hardly anyone on the road. It's really late. In fact, the dark sky is just starting to turn light in the east. As we cruise into my street the only things moving are the automatic sprinklers on some of the lawns.

"Thanks for taking me along tonight," I tell him as we pull up in front of my house.

"Glad to have you," Stu says with a yawn.

"How'd you do in the game?"

"Not bad, won a hundred and fifty."

"Sounds pretty good."

Stu shrugs. "I'll probably lose it all tomorrow night."

A thought comes to me and I grin. "We didn't talk much about Alix."

Stu raises a sleepy eyebrow. "You want to . . . now?"

I shake my head. "Naw, maybe there's really nothing to say."

"Seemed like you met a nice girl tonight."

"Yeah, but she'll be going back to Ohio in another month."

"Could be just what you need."

"Could be," I tell him, and pull the door open. I get out and watch Stu drive wearily away. The Cordoba kind of weaves down the street, but I know Stu didn't have anything to drink, so he's doing it on purpose. I turn and walk slowly up the slate path to my house. It's getting lighter out now and there's a thick blanket of dew on the lawn. For some reason I really wish tonight wouldn't end. I wish that Stu would just drive around the block and then come back and take me on another adventure. As I get closer to the front door I actually glance back toward the street, as if hoping that old Cordoba might reappear. Suddenly the last thing I want to do is go inside and get in bed and tomorrow go back to the same old life of cutting lawns and parking cars.

CHAPTER 30

The radio alarm clock next to my bed says 1:50 and my room is filled with bright sunshine. In ten minutes I'm going to be late for work. I can't believe I'm lying here on my bed still wearing the jeans and shirt I wore last night (never did get under the covers). I can't believe I stayed up all night talking to Lauren. I can't believe that I'm not going to be on time for work. But I'm not. And I'm not sure I care.

You know what I figured out before I fell asleep? For two years I was Alix Shuman's puppet. For two years I played a role. I worked hard. I parked cars. I cut lawns. I was saving money so I could buy a car that The Cold One would allow me to park in her carport. For two years I was the model boyfriend. Mr. Nice Guy. The son Big Phil the Nissan King wished he'd had. For two years I haven't really been me.

The more I think about it, the more I wonder if Alix ever really loved me. I think maybe she loved someone I pretended to be. But that person wasn't me. That person was someone safe to pass the time with until she grew up and went to college. I probably could have continued playing the role of the model boyfriend right through senior year, except that I got sick of it. And then I blew it with Paula. I started rumors. I tarnished Alix's image. So she had to get rid of me.

In a way I feel pretty bad for Alix because I tricked her. She liked me because I was one person, and then I changed into another. Not exactly from Dr. Jekyll to Mr. Hyde, but still enough of a change to make it hard for her. After all, she has to report to Big Phil and The Cold One. I may have been Alix's puppet for a couple of years, but she's been their puppet since the day she was born. Now I can understand why Shawn doesn't want anything to do with the Great Shuman Empire. Big Phil would probably have him spend his summers as an apprentice salesman in his used-car lot.

1:55. I love it. In five minutes I'm going to be late for work for the first time in my life. You know what was great about last night? I really had fun. I mean, I'm still not thrilled with the idea of Stu taking a hundred dollars off Frank, but hanging around the poker game was fun. And then staying up all night talking with Lauren. That was great. It really was. I can think of one other day this summer that I had fun—the day Paula and I went fishing. And the rest of the time? I was either working or with Alix. Looking back on it, I'm not sure there was a difference.

2:10. The phone downstairs is ringing. Bet you a hundred bucks it's one of the guys calling to see where the hell I am. It's not unusual that I'd be late, it's unheard of. They probably think that I've been killed in a car accident or something. The phone stops after two rings. The answering machine must have intercepted it. Sorry, guys, I hate to make you worry, but I'm just not in the mood to get up and explain why I'm here and not there.

After a while I do get up and take a shower and go downstairs to have breakfast. (I have recently invested in my own private supply of Pop-Tarts.) I'm in the middle of my third strawberry tart and thinking about how I'm going to spend the day when I happen to look out the window and see two cop cars in front of the Finkel house.

What's going on? I don't know, but it doesn't take me long to get dressed and go out to take a look.

Things seem pretty quiet outside the house, but as I go up the slate walk I notice that there are drops of blood on the gray stone. I knock on the front door and it's opened by a thin cop in a blue uniform. He gives me a funny look. "Yeah?"

"Uh, I live next door," I tell him. "I just wanted to see if everything is okay." As I say this I look into the living room and see Paula and another cop sitting on a couch.

Paula sees me too. "Oh, Scott, come in."

When the cop at the door hears this, he lets me through. As I step into the house I notice that there's a big brownish-red stain on the beige carpet near the door. I also glance into the kitchen. It looks like someone spilled dark red paint on the floor and then didn't do such a good job of mopping it up. It doesn't take a genius to figure out that the stain on the carpet and the red stuff on the kitchen floor is blood. But whose?

I look back at Paula. Not hers, or she wouldn't be sitting on the couch. Weird thoughts flash through my mind. Did Paula kill her mother? Or Eddie? But Paula doesn't look like she killed anyone. "Scott, this is Officer Douglas," she says, gesturing to the heavy red-faced cop sitting on the couch with her. "And that's Officer DiBartni."

"DiBartini," says the cop who let me in and is now standing behind me.

"Is everything okay?" I ask.

"Mom passed out and hurt her head this morning. It really wasn't as bad as it looks. But she got a big cut in her scalp and it bled all over the place. We had to take an ambulance to the hospital. Didn't you hear the sirens?"

"This morning?" I ask.

Paula nods. It's weird. Now that she's mentioned it, maybe I did hear something. But I'd only been in bed a couple of hours and I guess I was more interested in my sleep.

"Is she gonna be all right?" I ask.

"They think so," Paula says. "They took X rays and the doctor said everything looked okay. But they want her to stay there for a while." As she says this I notice the two cops glance at each other. DiBartini turns to me.

"You say you're the next-door neighbor?"

"Yeah."

"We called before. No one answered."

"I was probably asleep."

The cop gives me another funny look and I add, "I have a night job."

DiBartini nods. "Your parents friends with Mrs. Finkel?"

"Well, we know her and Paula," I reply diplomatically.

"You think I could talk to one of your parents?" he asks.

"Right now?"

The cop nods. "Yeah, right now."

"I guess."

"There's a phone in the den," Paula says, getting up. As we follow her I notice that the house has this musty smell, like no one's opened the windows in years. And the carpet's covered with all kinds of stuff besides blood. There are crumbs and candy wrappers and cigarette burns.

In the den Paula points to the phone and I pick it up and dial the club where my mother teaches tennis. I have to wait while they page her out on the tennis court.

Finally I hear her pick up the phone. "Scott? What is it?"

"Uh, I'm at the Finkels' and there's a policeman here who wants to talk to you."

"Why? What's wrong?"

"Uh, nothing, Mom. Here, talk to him." I hand the phone to Officer DiBartini, but before he talks to my mother, he turns to Paula and me.

"Why don't you two wait in the living room?"

Paula and I go out while DiBartini talks to my mother. We wind up standing near the glass doors that lead to the terrace and the pool. It's sunny out and Paula gazes at the raft, floating empty on the blue water. She's got that hard look on her face again, like she doesn't feel anything. But I know she must.

"You know what they're talking about?" I ask.

"Maybe he's asking if I can stay at your house until they talk to my father," Paula says. "They've been trying to call him all morning, but no one's been home."

"You think you'll be able to stay with him?"

"I hope." She crosses her arms in front of her and seems to

shiver. "God, I hope they don't send me to some kind of foster home."

"They won't," I tell her.

Paula just shrugs. "I'll be back in a second," she says, and heads toward the back of the house where her room is.

After she leaves, I realize that I can just barely hear DiBartini in the den on the telephone with my mother: "We're in a funny situation, Mrs. Tauscher. It's true her mother fell down and hurt her head, but from the looks of things and what Paula tells us, she's a pretty bad lush. . . . No, we don't know how long she's gonna be in the hospital, but now that we know the situation, it's not like we can just let her come back here and start living with the kid again. . . . Well, nine out of ten times the social services department winds up putting them in a foster home. . . . Mr. Finkel? That depends on whether he wants her. . . . What? Oh, you'd be surprised, Mrs. Tauscher."

They talk a bit more and then DiBartini calls to me. I pretend not to hear him so he won't suspect I've been listening.

"Scott," he says again. "Come in here. Your mother wants to talk to you."

I go back into the den and get on the phone. "Mom?"

"Scott, I only have a second and then I've got to get back to my lesson," she says. "Now, listen. It's fine for Paula to stay with us for as long as she wants. But for tonight I wasn't planning on coming home until late because there's a surprise anniversary party for Jack and Mary in the city. Your father is going to meet me there, and Kerry is staying at Andrea's. You better have Paula stay in Kerry's room and tomorrow we'll fix up a cot for her. And I don't know what's in the refrigerator, so maybe you ought to take her for dinner someplace. We should be home by twelve. You sure you'll be okay?"

"Sure, Mom."

I expect her to hang up, but she doesn't. "Well, I guess I owe you an apology. You were right about her mother."

"Don't sweat it, Mom."

"All right, I won't."

I hang up and the cops and I walk back out to the living room, where Paula is waiting for us. We all notice that she's put makeup on and is smoking a cigarette. I can't decide whether it's weird or not, considering what else is going on, but I can tell that the cops are a little surprised. But they also seem pretty eager to go and they quickly say good-bye.

After they leave, the house feels very quiet and empty.

"That was strange," I tell Paula.

Paula exhales a long stream of smoke. "They've been babysitting for me since nine this morning. I think they wanted to get some lunch."

That's her tough-girl act talking and I don't know how to reply. For a few moments we just stand in the living room. Everything looks dusty and dirty, so unlike your typical suburban home. Paula looks around and shudders.

"I just hope I'll never have to live here again," she says.

I nod and remember what DiBartini said. *Nine out of ten wind up in foster homes.*

"I'm sure your father will want you to come down there," I tell her.

Paula doesn't answer. She's looking away from me.

"Don't you think he will?" I ask.

Paula turns and looks up at me with tears in her eyes. "I don't know," she says in a suddenly frightened voice. "I don't know what I'm going to do if he doesn't want me. I can't stay here. I can't stay at your house forever. Where am I going to go?"

She turns away again and starts to sob. Until this moment, she'd done a good job of damming up her feelings. But now they all flood out. She's scared and I can't say I blame her. I watch as she wipes her eyes with her hand, smearing all the makeup she's just put on.

"Of course your father's going to want you," I tell her.

Paula shakes her head. She seems really agitated. "How do you know, Scott?" she asks. "Maybe he won't. Maybe he's too busy with his new wife and kids. What if I call and he's in a bad mood, or he just doesn't understand over the phone? What if he and Randy are having a fight, or one of the kids is sick?"

Before I can answer, she turns and rushes toward the back of the house again. "Paula? What are you doing?"

"Leaving," she yells back.

Oh, this is just wonderful. Here I am, supposedly taking care of her until my parents get home tonight and she decides she's leaving. I walk down the hall to her room and look in. Paula is pulling clothes out of her drawers and throwing them into a light blue suitcase on her bed.

"Paula, you're not serious."

"Wanna bet?" she says as she pulls open another drawer.

"I told my mother I'd take care of you."

Paula stops and stares at me. "Your mother can go to hell. And so can Officer DiBartini and everyone else in this world. They're not putting me in a foster home."

"You heard him?" I ask.

Paula nods and pulls several pairs of jeans out of her closet and dumps them into the suitcase.

"Where are you going to go?" I ask.

"I'll go to my father's first, and if he doesn't want me, I'll go someplace else."

"How will you get there?"

She just keeps packing and doesn't answer.

"Paula?"

"I'll hitchhike."

"Are you crazy? All the way to North Carolina? You can't."

"Try and stop me."

CHAPTER 31

Dear Mom and Dad,
    I'm driving Paula to North Carolina, BUT DON'T WORRY. Everything is fine. It's just that Paula was going to run away and I couldn't let her. I'm sure her father will let her stay there, but Paula wants to talk to him in person.
    Like I said, everything is OKAY. The van should make it and I'll call you tonight after you get home from the party.

Love, Scott

P.S. Dad, I borrowed $100 in case of emergency. Mom, I took some food.

I wanted another adventure, right? So here we are, tooling down the New Jersey Turnpike on our way to North Carolina. Paula has calmed down since we left her house, but I'm secretly wondering if I've gone nuts. Paula didn't make me do this, I volunteered. My parents are probably going to kill me, Stu is probably going to kill me, the cops may even kill me. But the funny thing is, I'm glad I'm doing it. For the first time in my life I'm on the open road, free of parents and bosses and everyone else who wants to tell me what to do. It's just me and Paula, making our own decisions, doing what we want to do for once. It feels pretty damn good.

The van is up to maximum cruising speed, 50 miles per hour, and we're stuck in the right lane getting passed by cars and trucks and everything else on this highway. In the back are a couple of suitcases with Paula's things, plus some blankets and a sleeping bag. In the front we have a shopping bag from my house filled with bread, peanut butter, jelly, fruit, pretzels, and some other goodies my mother hasn't gotten around to banning yet. I hope the note I left explains everything. In another hour we'll stop at a pay phone and try to call Paula's father again.

But for now it's just us and the highway. The road sounds and wind rush through the open windows (we're past the smelly part of New Jersey) and a ZZ Top tape is blasting out of Paula's portable tape player on the floor between us. All I can say is I feel great. It's like I just broke out of prison or something. Free of the chains that bound me. North Carolina, here we come.

We just passed the turnoff for the Pennsylvania Turnpike. Paula's looking through a shoe box full of tapes in her lap.

"Don't you want to know how my mother fell?" she asks.

"I thought she passed out," I answer.

"Eddie and I overslept this morning. She came in and found us."

"Uh-oh."

"You wouldn't believe it. She started screaming and ran out of the room. Then we heard a crash in the kitchen and when we got there she was out cold on the floor and bleeding. You know what Eddie did?"

"Fainted?"

Paula shakes her head. "He ran out of the house and left me there alone."

"A brave guy, Eddie."

"At first I was so scared. I called the operator and told her that my mother was bleeding to death on the kitchen floor. Then I ran out of the house to look for a police car. Then I ran back into the house and called the police. I called the fire department too. But you know what was weird, Scott?"

"What?"

"When the ambulance finally arrived, they came in and looked at my mother and told me they didn't think she was that badly hurt. They put all these bandages on her head and put her on a stretcher. I just stood there and watched. I felt numb. Like I didn't even care. My own mother. She could have been dead for all I knew."

"But you knew she wasn't badly hurt."

"But I was really hoping she was," Paula says. "I really hoped she'd die."

I feel goose bumps rise on my arms and back.

"Do you think that's sick?" she asks.

A big truck flies past us in the next lane and I have to hold on to the steering wheel to keep the van from being blown off the road. "No, I've thought the same thing too. And my parents never did anything compared to your mother. I remember wishing once that they'd die in a car accident just because they wouldn't let me go to a party."

"Really?"

"Yeah. The funny thing was, I felt so bad for thinking it that I decided they were right and I didn't deserve to go to the party. Not only that, but to pay penance I spent the night straightening up my room without being told to."

"I thought I was the only person in the world who wished her mother would die," Paula says.

"A lot of kids probably do. The only difference is, you have a better reason than most."

Just past the exit for Philadelphia we pull into a rest area and Paula goes to call her father while I put gas in the van. So far my baby's held up pretty well, but when the pump jockey checks the oil, there's hardly any in the crankcase.

"You need a couple of quarts," he tells me, holding up the dry dipstick.

It's a bad sign. I just put in two quarts last week. I tell him to put in the oil and then get down on my knees and look under the engine. Sure enough, it's dripping out of the bottom faster than before. I actually feel a pang of sadness. The end is approaching. I get up and pat the van gently on her side. Just get us down to North Carolina, I whisper. Then you can rest.

To be on the safe side I buy two extra quarts of oil and put them in back.

Paula comes out of the rest area smiling. "I talked to Randy. She said it was fine. I can stay as long as I want. You can stay too. But she said we shouldn't try to drive all the way there today. It's too far. We should stop someplace overnight and finish the trip tomorrow."

I glance at the van and back at Paula. "Well, let's keep going and see how far we can get tonight."

It's starting to get dark. We've been on the road now for almost six hours (passed Washington, D.C. about an hour ago). What Paula doesn't know is this is the longest I've ever driven in my life. I can feel it too. The muscles in my shoulders are starting to knot up and ache. A lot of it must be tension. I've had to put two fresh quarts of oil in the van since Philadelphia. And the leak is getting worse.

Paula has decided that if her father and Randy will let her she's going to stay in North Carolina and go to school there. I guess she figures that now that the police know her mother drinks she has a pretty good case for staying with her dad.

It's getting darker. I switch on the van's lights and we roll up the windows and Paula pulls on a bright red sweatshirt. My shoulders are really killing me.

"Hey, Paula, you think you could climb around behind me and massage my shoulders a little?"

"Sure." She climbs over the front seat and crouches behind me, rubbing and kneading my aching shoulder muscles.

"You think we should stop soon?" she asks.

"I want to keep going for a while more," I tell her. The truth is, I wouldn't mind stopping, but where? Since we passed Washington, it's been pretty much dark highway. I know we're in

Virginia, but I've never been here before. Are we allowed to park in a rest area and sleep? Or do we have to get off the highway and find a place? Until I can figure out the answer, I guess we might as well keep going.

Nine o'clock. Ten o'clock. Eleven. The minutes and hours grind by as the highway slips under the front wheels and is spewed out the back. The music's off and all we hear is the steady grating sound of the road as we grind out mile after mile. The empty pretzel bag is on the floor and the ashtray is full of Paula's butts. Next to me Paula yawns and gives me a nervous look.

"You sure you're not too tired?" she asks for the sixth time.

"I'm okay," I tell her, even though my eyesight is getting a little blurry and my right foot has been on the gas pedal so long that it feels like it's falling asleep.

"Maybe we ought to stop soon," Paula says.

"Sure." Maybe we'll come across a sign that will say: Warm cozy beds. Free for teenaged runaways and their friends.

After midnight, outside Richmond, Virginia, we stop at a self-service station along the highway. When we get out of the van to stretch our stiff bodies, the air smells different. Much more countryish. The night seems darker here than it does up in New York. Out on the highway the big trucks roar by, but under the lights of the service station everything seems still. Paula and I look at each other and I can tell she feels the difference too.

I check the oil and put in two more quarts. It seems to drip out the bottom almost as fast as I put it in. But maybe it only does that when we're standing still. Next to me Paula stretches and yawns. I go into the office, which smells of oil and cigarettes and reminds me of the Texaco where Eddie hung out. Only in this office there's a big fat guy in dirty overalls smoking a cigarette and watching a tiny TV set on his desk. He's got a thick Fu Manchu mustache and long dirty-blond hair pulled into a ponytail behind his back.

"Know a place where me and my friend can stay for the night?" I ask as I pay him for the gas and oil.

The guy looks up from the TV and out the window at Paula. He smiles. "They ain't gonna let you stay in no motel around here, son," he says with a southern drawl. "You best off sleepin' in your truck."

"Just anywhere?" I ask.

He thinks for a moment and then shakes his head. His jowls jiggle like Jell-O. "Tell you what you do, son. You go on down the highway 'bout three exits. Make a right off the ramp an' follow that road 'bout five miles. You'll see some picnic tables on the right. Should be okay there."

That's good news. "Thanks," I tell him.

He nods. "Next time tell her to bring along a friend," he says, and winks.

Back in the van I tell Paula that we don't have far to go.

"Good," she says, "because I'm really tired."

But back on the highway the three exits the pump jockey was talking about aren't exactly bunched together. There's a lot of dark road to cover first. And now the van is starting to misfire and lose power.

"What's wrong with it, Scott?" Paula asks as we lurch and sputter along.

"I'm not sure, maybe it's just tired." A pretty lame answer, but the best I can come up with under the circumstances. Meanwhile we're down to forty-five miles per hour.

"Could you look out the back and tell me what color the exhaust is?" I ask, wondering if we're burning oil, in which case the exhaust would be white.

Paula climbs over the seat and goes to the back of the van and looks out the rear window. "I can't see the exhaust," she says, "but the sparks are kind of orangish."

Sparks? I have no idea what that means. If the muffler had fallen down and we were dragging it, we'd hear the engine. God, I'm so tired, I don't want to stop and check it out. All I want to do is make it to that place the pump jockey told me about.

Pretty soon we're down to forty miles per hour. But we've

passed two exits and I'm praying the third will come up soon. Finally I see it in the distance. The exit speed is posted at thirty-five, but we couldn't go faster if we wanted to. We get on the road from the highway. Five miles to go.

"Now there are lots of sparks," Paula says from the back.

Lots of sparks?

The van holds steady at thirty-five miles per hour as we lumber and backfire down this dark road. There's not another car coming in either direction. Nothing but telephone poles and trees. We cover one mile, then another, then another. Suddenly the van starts misfiring badly and we slow to twenty-five miles per hour. Something's really wrong now. Every warning light on the dashboard is lit up bright red and the headlights are starting to fade.

"The sparks are gone," Paula says from the back.

Whew!

"Now there are flames coming out."

"What? How big?"

"How big are what?" Paula asks.

"How big are the flames?"

"I don't know. A couple of feet, I guess."

Flames mean fire. And I just filled the gas tank.

"Paula, get ready to get out," I yell. The van's headlights are just about gone now, but it doesn't matter because I'm pulling off the road and stopping. The van quickly fills with smoke, but Paula and I jump out even quicker.

As soon as we're out of the van I grab her hand and we run. "Come on! It could explode!"

In the dark we run down the road shoulder, the gravel crunching under our feet. About thirty yards away we stop and look back. Smoke is billowing out of the back of the van and red sparks are falling to the ground under the engine compartment. But there are no flames anymore. And so far it hasn't exploded.

Paula and I look at each other in the dark and then look around. The first thing I notice are the stars. I've never seen so many. There's no moon tonight, just stars. Millions and millions of them, twinkling, shimmering, glowing. The land around us is flat. It's hard to tell what's out there because it's so dark. And we can hear things. Things going *peep-peep-peep*, things that sound like crickets, and things making noises we've never heard before. But I don't feel as scared as I thought I would. It seems too peaceful out here.

After a while the smoke pretty much stops and there are no more sparks falling from the engine compartment. I figure it's safe to take a look. Paula and I walk around to the back of the van and I pull up the engine cover. A puff of smoke rises out of it, revealing what's left of the engine, still glowing a faint, darkening red. It looks like mechanical rigor mortis has set in. My van, my baby, has gone to the big junkyard in the sky.

"Will it go anymore?" asks Paula.

I shake my head.

"What should we do?"

"Go to sleep and try to call your father in the morning," I tell her. "I have a feeling we're not far from North Carolina."

CHAPTER 32

The safest place to spend the night is inside the van. After we open the windows and doors to let the smoke out, it doesn't smell too bad. Just slightly burnt. The only light we have is a couple of matches, which Paula holds while I lay out the sleeping bag and blankets. I tell Paula to take the bag.

We lock the doors, but crack the windows for fresh air, and lie down. As tired as we are, sleep seems a long way off. The floor of the van is hard, and maybe we're still a little nervous about being out in the middle of nowhere. Lying close to each other in the dark must have something to do with it too.

"Scott?"

"Yeah?"

"Are you mad?"

"About what?"

"The engine melting."

"No. It was bound to happen sooner or later. I'm just glad the van got to see some of this great United States before she passed away."

Paula giggles. Next to her, wrapped in the blankets, I'm aware of every inch of my body on the side bordering her sleeping bag. The floor is so hard that both of us turn and squirm to find comfortable positions. But each time we touch accidentally, we jump back.

"You never said good-bye to Eddie," I tell her.

"I don't care if I never see him again."

"Because of what happened this morning?"

"I haven't really liked him for weeks. It's just, uh, sometimes it's hard to break up."

"Like me and Alix," I tell her. "We probably should have broken up a long time ago. But you get used to being with a person, even after the two of you really don't care about each other anymore."

Paula doesn't answer, but I know that if I could see in the dark she'd be nodding in agreement. It's weird. We've gone through two different experiences, but somehow we've wound up in the same place.

The sleeping bag scrapes on the van's floor as Paula turns around, trying to find a comfortable position. We talk for a while and then turn over and try to sleep. But then one of us hears the other turning and trying to find a more comfortable spot and we start talking again.

"You know, Scott," Paula says. "If I can really stay with my father, I'm going to start all over again new. Maybe I'll buy all new clothes. Things that aren't so flashy. People judge you so much on the clothes you wear."

Something about the way she says that makes me smile. She really is a cute kid in some ways. I half feel like rolling over and hugging her.

"Will you ever come down and visit me, Scott?"

"Sure."

"I really feel like you're my friend now."

"Yeah."

"You're the only person I can really talk to."

"Yeah?"

"Scott?" There's something in her voice. We're both on our sides, facing each other. It's so dark I can't tell how far away her face is. But I can feel her near me.

"Yeah?"

"Would you hold me? Just for a little while?"

"Sure." I slide over and find that she's farther away than I thought. I put my arms around the sleeping bag with her inside it. Then I pull her close. Her head is just below my chin.

"I really feel bad about my mother," she whispers.

"Don't worry, she'll be okay. Maybe now that this has happened she'll get some help."

"I really don't hate her," Paula whispers. "I'm just afraid of her."

I reach up and pat her head.

"I'm afraid she's going to come and make me go back with her."

"Don't worry about that now," I whisper, holding her tighter.

"Scott?"

"Yeah?"

"Do you want to come into the sleeping bag with me?"

It's amazing how a few words can affect you. A second ago I wasn't even thinking of it. I was just holding her like I'd hold Kerry if she ever needed it. But no sooner do I hear those words than my temperature must rise five degrees and my body starts to tingle. Here it is finally, the most golden of golden opportunities: an open invitation, a whole night together, no parents around, no one to bother us. In my mind I'm already in the sleeping bag with her. In my mind my hands are already undressing her. In my mind . . . in my mind . . . in my mind . . .

"No." I slide away from her.

"Why?"

How can I explain it? "I just can't," I tell her. "I mean, I can, but I shouldn't. I mean, I want to, but if you really want to start all over again, then I don't want to. I mean, you really do want to start all over again, don't you?"

Paula is quiet for a moment. Then I hear her whisper, "Yes."

"Then you know this isn't the way to do it."

For a while we don't talk. The air in the van is quiet. The insides of the windows are sooty from the smoke, but I can still see through them to the stars outside. Am I the world's biggest fool? Could Paula understand that I just gave up the first great golden opportunity of my life because I care too much about her? Jeez, she's so quiet and still. I'm worried that she might feel like I've rejected her or something.

"Maybe I ought to go sleep outside," I tell her.

"Don't," she says.

"Paula, you gotta promise me you'll never tell anyone about this," I tell her, thinking of the guys back home.

"I won't."

"I don't want you to think I was afraid to, or anything."

"I don't, silly."

"Well, you know."

"Maybe you're right, Scott. If I'm really going to change, I might as well start now."

"I guess." Will I live to regret this? I wonder.

"Night, Scott."

"Night, Paula."

CHAPTER 33

In a couple of minutes this jet I'm on is going to land at LaGuardia Airport. Mr. Finkel gave me the money for the flight back from North Carolina. I called my mother and she said one of the guys would be waiting for me. She wasn't sure which one. But wait, I'm getting ahead of myself. Let me tell you what happened first.

I guess we finally did fall asleep in the van, but early the next morning we were awakened by someone knocking on the door. I pulled it open and there was a North Carolina State Trooper outside. I explained how the van had broken down and about the wooded place with the picnic tables we were trying to get to. The trooper laughed. He said it was true that if we'd gone another couple of miles we would have found a wooded place with some picnic tables. But right behind those tables was the state trooper barracks.

Anyway, Paula and I packed up our things and I took the license plates off the van. The trooper gave us a ride down to the barracks. They called Mr. Finkel for us.

It turned out that we were still a couple of hours from Raleigh, and it took Mr. Finkel a while to drive up and get us. He pulled up in the same silver Caddy I saw in Paula's driveway. Except instead of wearing a jogging outfit, he was wearing a suit and tie. Paula literally jumped into his arms when she saw him. I could tell he was pretty glad to see her too. I waited until they were finished hugging and then Paula introduced me. Mr. Finkel thanked me for bringing Paula down and said he was sorry about my van. I was impressed. He didn't even give me the evil eye about spending the night with her or anything.

I stayed in Raleigh with Mr. Finkel and Randy for three days. Randy was really nice. They had two young kids; one was two and a half, and the other about ten months. Paula went crazy over them. She said she'd love to baby-sit and help take care of them. I think Mr. Finkel and Randy were glad to have Paula come live there, but getting a free baby-sitter and part-time househelper sure didn't hurt.

I couldn't tell much about Raleigh during the time I was there. Mostly we hung around the house, which had plenty of room for everyone. When we did go out, it struck me that the people were slower and easier-going than up north. The city of Raleigh is a lot smaller than New York, obviously. This may sound corny, but it seems more wholesome too. If Paula really is going to change, this is probably a good place to try it.

I know that Paula and her father had a couple of long talks while I was down there. Mr. Finkel even had a talk with me this morning before he and Paula drove me to the airport. He asked about Mrs. Finkel. I guess he just wanted to make sure what Paula told him was true. Of course, I didn't say anything about Eddie.

When I get off the plane, Gordy and Albert are waiting for me. It's only noon. They've got two hours until work begins.

"Hey, there he is!" Gordy yells.

Albert slaps me on the back. "Didn't know you had it in you, man."

"Had what in me?" I ask.

Albert looks a little surprised. "Well, uh, running away with Paula Finkel. Everyone knows."

"What are you guys talking about?" I ask as we walk down to

the baggage claim area. "I didn't run away with her. I just took
her down to her father's place in North Carolina."

Albert and Gordy glance at each other. "We heard the troop-
ers nailed you."

"They didn't nail us. They picked us up when the van died."

"Didn't Paula attack her mother with a hammer?" Gordy
asks.

I can only shake my head. What incredible rumors.

"Then how come her old lady's in the hospital with a concus-
sion?" Albert asks.

"She fell down and hurt her head."

"That's all?" Gordy asks.

"Sorry to disappoint you."

We get down to the baggage area. There's a lot of luggage and
stuff going around the carousel, but only one bundle that consists
of a sleeping bag and two blankets wrapped around a pair of
license plates. I grab it and we head out toward the parking lot.

Gordy's looking at his watch. "Guess we better go straight to
work."

"Can you drop me off at my house?" I ask. We've arrived at
Albert's car, but neither Gordy nor Albert gets in. They stand on
the other side, looking across the roof at me.

"You know you've missed four days," Albert says. "Stu's kind
of expecting you."

"I'm not going back to work," I tell him.

"What?" Albert scowls.

"I said I'm not going back to work."

"What are you gonna do for money?" Gordy asks.

"I've got some saved."

"I thought that was for new wheels," Albert says.

"I'm just gonna get another used van."

"Jeez, what's with you?" Albert asks.

"Nothing. Except I'm taking the rest of the summer off," I
tell him. "First summer in five years."

"What are you gonna do?" Gordy asks.

"I don't know. Hang around, go fishing, stay up late, chase
girls. Basically I'm gonna do whatever I feel like doing."

Albert and Gordy both look like they don't know what to say. We get in the car and start to drive home. I can't ever remember driving anywhere with these guys without someone talking about something. But today we go in silence. All the way to the driveway of my house.

Then Gordy leans over the front seat. "You know, your parents are gonna kill you."

"Shut up, stupid," Albert snaps. Then he looks across the seat at me. "I don't blame you, man," he says.

AFTERWORD

My parents didn't kill me. In fact, they pretty much understood. I told them I'd keep a couple of my gardening jobs in order to make some spending money. Otherwise I'm just taking it easy. I figure this is my last chance to take some time off because next year I'll graduate from high school and probably work all summer to save money for college.

After I got home, I looked in the phone book, and just like Lauren said, there was only one Wax listed. I called and she was there. We've started going out pretty steadily. In fact, I think I've seen her just about every night since I got back from North Carolina.

A couple of nights ago we were leaving Cook's when I saw the Benz pull up. Alix was driving and there was a guy in the passenger seat. I didn't recognize him; he looked older, probably in college. Alix saw me with Lauren too. It was weird, and I'd be lying if I didn't admit that I felt a little jealous. But as we passed each other in the parking lot Alix kind of smiled and I kind of smiled back. I guess we both knew there were no hard feelings. The time had just come to move along.

ABOUT THE AUTHOR

Todd Strasser's most recent books for Delacorte Press were *Turn It Up!* and *The Complete Computer Popularity Program*. *Friends Till the End* and *Rock 'n' Roll Nights* were named American Library Association Best Books for Young Readers and are, along with *Angel Dust Blues* and *Workin' for Peanuts*, available in Dell Laurel-Leaf editions. He lives in New York City with his wife and daughter.